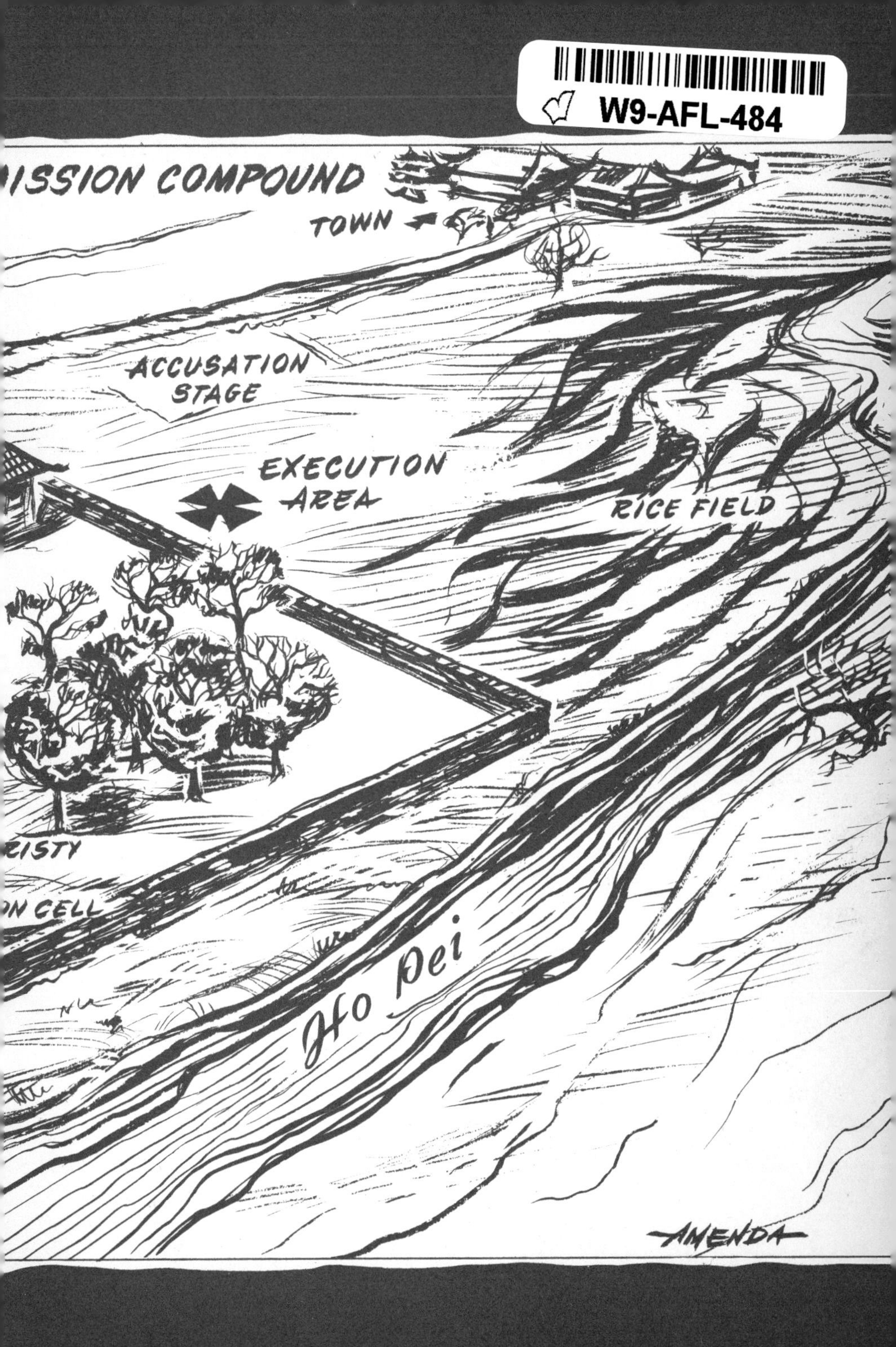
ISSION COMPOUND
TOWN
ACCUSATION
STAGE
EXECUTION
AREA
RICE FIELD
RISTY
ON CELL
Ho Pei
AMENDA

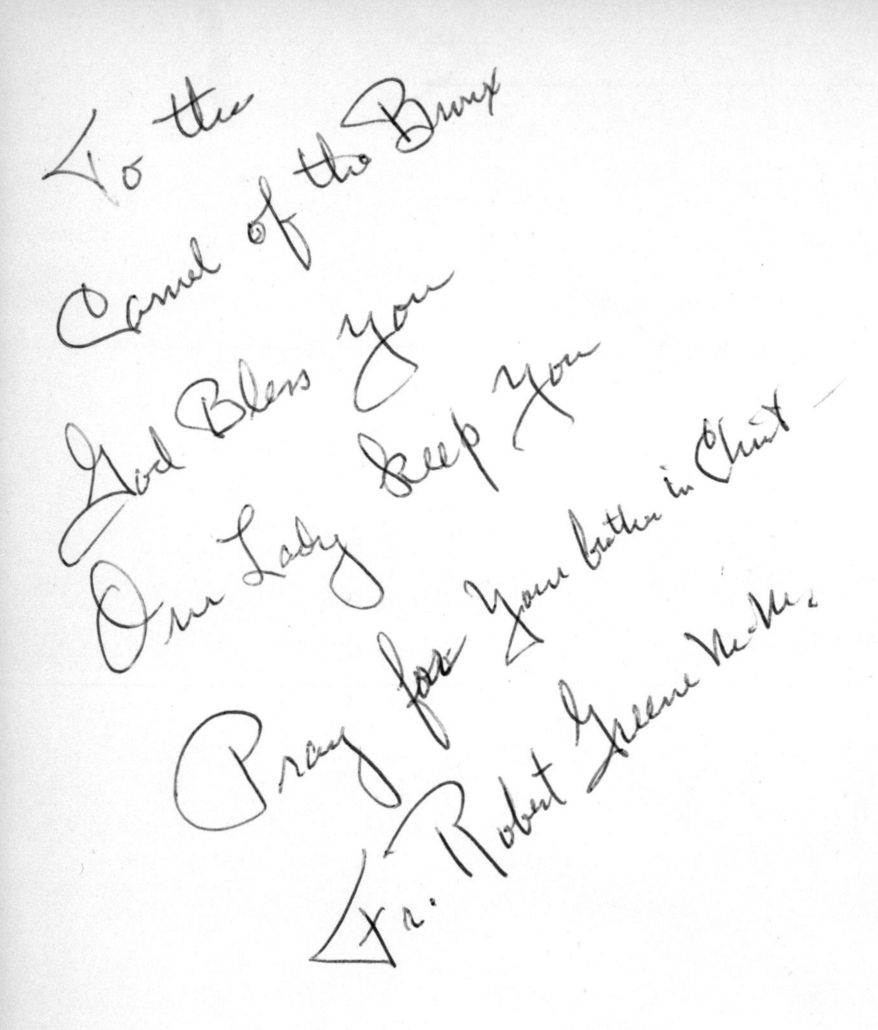

To the
Carmel of the Bronx
God Bless you
Our Lady keep you
Pray for your brother in Christ
Fr. Robert Greene [illegible]

CALVARY IN CHINA

CALVARY IN CHINA

Rev. Robert W. Greene, M.M.

G. P. Putnam's Sons New York

Published on the same day in the Dominion of Canada
by Thomas Allen, Ltd., Toronto.

Library of Congress Catalog Card Number: 53-5326

Second Impression

MANUFACTURED IN THE UNITED STATES OF AMERICA

VAN REES PRESS • NEW YORK

In humble gratitude
these pages are dedicated
to Mary,
The Virgin Mother of Our Lord.

Acknowledgment

WITH heartfelt gratitude I wish to make acknowledgment of the debt I owe my confrere, Rev. John F. Donovan, M.M., a veteran Maryknoll Missioner in South China, for his precious contribution in making this book a reality.

When I returned to the United States it was Father Donovan who took me in hand and with kindly but firm insistence led me to dictate the first draft of this manuscript. With limitless patience, then, he reviewed each facet of its complex story, checked with authorities on each detail that required corroboration, and with truly fraternal solicitude guided me in the apt expression of inner thoughts that I felt loath and unqualified to put on paper.

Contents

CALVARY IN CHINA

CHAPTER ONE

Our Friend, Leang Fan

YOUNG MR. LEANG FAN was a popular teacher in the village school in Tung-an in South China. Although he was not a Christian, of all the young men in Tung-an he would call most frequently at the mission to visit us.

It was good to see him coming briskly along the path toward the house we used for our temporary rectory. Leang Fan was always neat and clean and, unlike the other young men in Tung-an, who were close-cropped, his hair was long and he parted it sharply in the middle of his round head. His skin was the color of the fresh local olives and just as smooth; it had never been darkened or coarsened by the hot sun in the fields. And when he smiled, his teeth showed white and even.

When I poured him a cup of tea, it sounded so genuine to hear him say: "Father, I'm not worthy to be served tea by *you.*" He'd rise and bow just right as he accepted the cup with both hands.

It is good, we used to say, to have young Mr. Leang Fan as our friend. He was a leader in the area, and in every group his calm voice dominated the talk. The people of the town respected him; and we felt certain he would not permit anyone to talk nonsense about us. The children in his school would hear from him favorable things about us—although we noticed that several times toward the end of the year 1949 the youngsters were not overly polite toward us.

Sometimes Mr. Leang Fan came in for some of our Western drugs (about which he understood a good deal) for one of his students; and at other times he came in just to sip tea and ask questions about life in America.

Leang Fan was a born storyteller. He had a fund of fantastic tales about animal life. He liked dogs as pets ("Just as you do," he'd add). He would tell us stories about the customs of his people, explaining Chinese history. Often he would make us uncomfortable when he belittled their ancient customs and ridiculed the dirt of the homes in Tung-an. He wanted to impress upon us that *he* was different—his education had made him understand that China needed change and must discard outmoded ways. "Gambling and other vices must be eliminated. Opium smoking must be wiped out," he'd say vehemently. He seemed to sense that we agreed with this wholeheartedly.

"Father," he would say, "you understand our local customs very well, and you speak like a native of China. The people of Tung-an, you know, think very highly of you and the other Fathers."

"You flatter us unduly," I would say, "but it makes us happy to hear you say such things. We like the people of Tung-an very much, and we do our best to help them. Perhaps the work in our dispensary has helped a bit to gain and keep their good will."

"Father, have you any news of the Church in other parts of China?" Leang Fan asked one day.

"No details," I said, "but we have heard that in the North things have gone very hard with the Christians and priests."

"Do you think the Communists will ever come to Tung-an?"

"Tung-an is a very small place," I said, "and it is doubtful that the Reds would bother us here. And furthermore, I don't think the people of Tung-an would ever accept Communism."

"I think you are quite right, Father," he said. "But," he added after a pause, "should they ever come, have you any plans? Where would you go?"

"No, no plans," I said, "except to stay here. We have done no harm to anyone so we have nothing to fear."

"But you do not approve of Communism, Father—isn't that correct?"

"Yes, that's quite right. We cannot approve of the atheistic philosophy of Russian Communism. All we would ask of the Red leaders—should they ever come to Tung-an—is that we be permitted to continue our work for the people; just to be left alone."

I remember how bitter he was in his remarks about Communism, and how he emphasized the point that there would be no real danger in Tung-an. "We are Kwangsi people," he would say somewhat arrogantly, "and we are a tough, proud people."

And with that I was in agreement one hundred per cent.

It made us feel good to hear young Mr. Leang Fan so confident about Tung-an, although my reason convinced me that Kwangsi could never hold out once the rest of China went Red.

For several weeks after that last chat our young teacher friend did not call at the mission, and we thought it rather strange. The next time we saw Leang Fan was under circumstances we could never have anticipated.

It was in the expectant silence of the early morning of December 5, 1949. The big mission-gate bell, whose soft resonance had an hour before struck the Angelus, was now clanging furiously like a piece of fire apparatus answering an alarm. I was just finishing my Mass, but Father Gilmartin, who was kneeling in the rear of the chapel, looked out and I could see by the stunned expression of his normally placid face that it was something more than the prank of some local youngsters. There was trouble.

Then the awful possibility flashed through my mind as I quickly unvested. Despite what Leang Fan had said, we had spoken among ourselves for weeks about the possibility of the Reds reaching Tung-an. After all, Kweilin, Nanning and all the large Kwangsi cities to the immediate north of us had fallen. So this must be it.

I went out the side door of the chapel and I saw a large number of armed men moving about the mission property. Approaching me along the walk that led from the rectory were three young men. They had large red cloth bands on their right arms, and they were carrying revolvers. In the middle of the three was our friend, young Mr. Leang Fan, a large red band on his right arm and a revolver in his hand. Our eyes met as the group of three passed silently by me, but he didn't seem to see me. My stomach went cold. I felt weak all over. It was like looking at a brother who had just betrayed a trust.

The soldiers I saw were all Kwangsi boys, armed with pistols and guns. About two hundred of them took over the town of Tung-an without using a bullet. Many of the people of the nearby villages didn't learn about the change in government until they came the next day to Tung-an for market. Then they found out that Tung-an was Red.

Like all of us the people had been expecting the Communists to take over, and like us they were fearfully awaiting an army from the North—strangers from outside. Schools had been closed for several weeks, children were kept at home, girls had been sent out of town to relatives back in the hills. No one would be safe along the bus route or in the market when the Red devils came from the North. Everyone seemed to be looking to the North; no one could see the Red army in the young men with whom they sat in the teahouse on market day. Communism had been in Tung-an but the armbands were kept out of sight until that morning in December 1949.

Late in the afternoon some days after this, I was in the dispensary taking care of an old lady. Two of the three Chinese Sisters attached to our mission were gathering flowers for the altar. A young Christian rushed excitedly into the dispensary and cried: "They're here!"

I asked: "Who are here?"

He said: "The army—the Red army. They are marching down the bus road."

I looked out and my eyes at once confirmed the man's statement.

I called Father Nugent and told him to remove the Blessed Sacrament from the Chapel and put It in our quarters. I then returned to the mission gate and watched the approaching army. There were about four thousand foot soldiers in perfect order marching four abreast. As they drew near the mission they broke up into smaller columns of about five hundred and swung off the bus road into the small paths that led to the various villages surrounding Tung-an. They all seemed to know exactly where they were going.

Those who passed by the mission gate did not so much as glance at me. They were extremely well disciplined and well equipped and well clothed. We had never before seen troops like this in China. They were different from our local fifth column that had so unexpectedly executed the coup d'état a few days before.

As they marched along in their orderly, easy stride they sang with zest and enthusiasm their rousing Communist songs—martial and lilting, not Chinese, but definitely Western in rhythm. They strode by with a proud, confident step, with the air of men who felt they were in very truth liberators of the people. And there was no need to fear these men. The children were safe on the streets, and the local women and girls were absolutely unmolested by them. It was immediately apparent that these were well-trained and highly disciplined troops. The next day a number of them came to the mission for medicine, and some of them told me of the days when they had fought under Stillwell in Burma. One recalled how U.S. medics had tended his wound in the Southwest when he was fighting against the Japanese.

A young soldier with paint and brush and large bold strokes wrote four Chinese characters on the mission wall near the gatehouse: *Tsung Chiao Tzu Yu*—Freedom of Religion.

Our Christians, seeing the words "Freedom of Religion" on the mission walls, came to Mass normally on Sundays and also to the dispensary for medicine, and things seemed to be going on as usual. The soldiers and officers did not bother us—in fact they were surprisingly friendly. However, this first wave of Red troops, these well-behaved, well-trained men, were not to remain long with us in Tung-an.

In January 1950 these fighting troops moved out, and a new wave of Red soldiers descended upon the town.

These men were not so well armed nor, we soon discovered, so well disciplined.

They had a different purpose from the strictly military men. We now had the propaganda teams with us—the indoctrinators, men and women whose duty it was to make every man, woman and child who was outside the fold in Tung-an a convert to Communism. Toward the end of January about thirty-five members of this group moved into the mission property.

I rushed out with Ah-Hiu, our cook, and asked the officer in charge why they were occupying the mission. He replied with feigned seriousness: "For your protection against the bandits. We do not want your property to fall into the hands of the guerrillas."

On our way back to the rectory, Ah-Hiu whispered: "Father, it isn't for *our* protection they have moved into the mission walls—but for their own. They are afraid of the powerful guerrilla forces."

I suspected that Ah-Hiu was right.

One night shortly after the occupation of the mission as I lay half awake on my bed with the moon flooding the room, I heard a strange, scraping, rhythmic shuffling of feet on the dirt road beneath the window. I looked out and felt a cold sweat come over me as I made out the forms of about twenty-five soldiers marching Indian fashion with a civilian at the head of the line. No spoken word came from the men as they passed on down the road toward the village of the Lees.

The next day on returning from the market our cook excitedly gave us the frightening news. "Old Lee Tu-pao," he said, "was taken from his home last night and no one knows what has happened to him."

Lee Tu-pao only a few months before had manifested sincere interest in the Church's doctrine, and in the village of the Lees we were planning to open a new catechumenate in the spring. All over the area an ominous fear had settled, and for the present there seemed no hope of a doctrine course anywhere.

These stealthy footsteps in the night under my window soon became familiar sounds. I would watch the silent figures march by in single file, always with a civilian at the head of the line. They would scrape along the dirt bus road and then bend off toward a village neighboring on Tung-an.

Our people of Tung-an wanted trouble with no one. They were extremely conservative peasants, honest and, when necessary, hard working. We had no wealthy families in our area, although some naturally were better off than others. They cultivated their fields and relaxed with their tea, and desired to be left at peace.

Tung-an means "mutual peace." It is a market town in our Maryknoll mission district in Kweilin in Southwest Kwangsi Province, about seven hundred miles west of Canton. My mission town nestled in the middle of a long, deep, fertile valley, about a mile and a half wide, with a clear swift stream cutting through the middle, where the women daily brought their clothes for washing. The mountains walling in the valley were terraced almost to the top with rice paddies reaching up to suck the springs and rain water that trickled down the sides.

Sometimes toward evening when I would be coming along the mountain paths, I'd hear the whirling of the water and the whining of the wind, and it would sound like prayers of petition going up for the people of Tung-an. Looking down from the top of these mountains the six compact villages in the valley beneath, each surrounded by its quilt of rice fields, made a picture of breathtaking beauty.

Our people were independent in their ways and in their thinking. They didn't want to be dominated by anyone. They could take care of their own local affairs, their own schools and their own laws. There was no prison or jail in the valley of

Tung-an; lawbreakers were punished on the spot or were sent to the county seat of Ping-lo.

These simple farmers, Christian and pagan, always greeted us pleasantly on the streets. All felt free to come to our dispensary; all received the same treatment. We were accepted. We were part of Tung-an.

There was a growing tenseness and uneasiness in the valley. There were now Red soldiers on our property, and we had heard rumors that they intended to take over the compound for use as a regional headquarters. Even though we sensed an increasingly unfriendly attitude on the part of the officials and soldiers, still we were (with permission, of course) allowed to carry on our mission work and visit our Christians. With the optimism of young missioners we still had hopes that the "Freedom of Religion" characters on our mission wall would prove more than mere words.

About this time, I recall, I went to Fragrant Flower Village, fifteen miles away. The head of the village was wise Grandfather Wu, one time catechist at the mission. His was one of the better homes of Fragrant Flower Village, but no one seemed to envy the Wus; they had always treated the other families justly and kindly. After our evening rice we sat around in the inner patio of the sprawling Wu home talking about the fields and the crops. Then suddenly and quietly Grandfather Wu asked about the Reds in our town of Tung-an. It was inevitable that we talk about Communism, but each one was reticent to introduce the topic.

A young man boasted: "The Reds may take over Tung-an, but they will never be able to rule over Fragrant Flower Village."

Old Wu looked at the younger man sagely and said: "It is true I have seen armies come and go, revolutions rise and fall.

Still, if the Communists have succeeded in taking over whole provinces and other towns and villages of Kwangsi, Fragrant Flower Village has no hope of holding out against them."

Then he turned encouragingly to me and said: "But, Father, you priests and we Catholics will not have any harm come to us. After all, China has over four hundred million people and we Catholics are a small, impotent minority. We have nothing to fear from the new regime."

I replied not overconfidently: "We can only pray and hope that it will be so."

Sensing my uncertainty for the Church's future, Grandfather Wu generously assured me: "If ever you should need a sanctuary in an hour of danger, you may depend on us to harbor you; and there is no one in Fragrant Flower Village who would betray you."

One of Wu's sons asked: "Father, do you think that you should return to America now that great danger has come to our area?"

"No," I replied. "We shall not leave Tung-an. You and the other Catholics are our spiritual children, and we must not leave our people no matter how grave the danger." They liked to hear that, remembering that we had remained with them during the trying days of World War II.

A week after I had visited the Wu family in Fragrant Flower Village, our cook excitedly came in after his trip to the market with the heartrending news that three Red soldiers had arrested Grandfather Wu that morning as he was preparing to come to Tung-an. The charge leveled at him was conspiracy against the People's Government, and co-operating with the guerrillas. Two weeks later he was put to death.

Despite some minor restrictions, however, we carried on our work. The dispensary was opened every day and large numbers of patients—including many Red soldiers—came for treatment. The Christians continued to come to Mass and the Sacraments, even though they knew this did not meet with the full approval of the new authorities. Or possibly they came to show their resolve to resist the oppression that had come over the area.

Certainly the people were not happy about the "liberation." They were not pleased with the new restrictions on their freedom of expression and movement. They were not happy about the rise in taxes, which came after the new government had promised that they would be decreased.

It was known, generally, that the guerrilla bands had increased during this time because of this feeling of resentment against the rulers from the North.

The Communists themselves later confided that though they had been in many parts of China, never had they before experienced such deep-seated hatred for the Liberation Army and the new People's Government. And they respected the guerrillas in our area and hesitated to engage them in a mountain battle.

When the August harvest was in, I approached the local officials for permission to visit some villages where we had Christians.

"We must refuse you," he said, "because the hills which you plan to visit are not safe for you."

"I am not afraid to go where there are bandits," I replied.

"That is what puzzles us," he said. "Why is it that you, unarmed and alone, dare walk among the bandits, and our soldiers hesitate to do so even in groups of ten and twelve?"

I explained that we priests have nothing of value to steal. "Our Mass kit is our only baggage," I said, "and if any bandit were to steal it everyone would know from whence it came."

Then I added: "My duty is to take care of my people. To

serve them and try to help them. Our mission in China is to 'do good'; we are certain that God will take care of us."

The permission, however, was not granted, and we began to feel the noose tightening around our activities. Ah-Hiu, our loyal cook, kept us informed of the Communist development; but every report he brought in seemed to confirm us in our fear that for the present, at least, we would not be free to leave the mission and carry on our preaching in distant villages.

CHAPTER TWO

Ah-Hiu, My Cook

OUR UNLOCKED DOORS put us at the mercy of everyone in Tung-an, curious to see the foreigners and their home. Soldiers and students would come in night and day. Sometimes they would enter the rooms to search for "unregistered visitors"; sometimes they would come to question us; more often they would come simply to annoy us.

The increasing strain soon began to tell on our nerves. The enforced inactivity, the uncertainty, the unwarranted suspicion, their growing hatred—all overwhelmingly oppressed us. We didn't want to talk about the prospects. We didn't want to talk. We thought about our twenty-one mission stations, far away and uncared for.

My nights were restless and often sleepless. I heard the eerie scraping of feet fade off toward another village and knew there was another victim; I'd think of the three Chinese Sisters and what might eventually happen to them; I'd think of our Christians, and wonder if all of them would be faithful and loyal. I'd finger my Rosary again, as I lay tossing on my rope bed, but my thoughts were not on my beads. It all seemed so unreal—my being here in Tung-an, thousands of miles from my Indiana home.

One sleepless night I recall smiling when I asked myself: "Did you ever think being a missioner would mean this?" I gave myself an answer I vaguely recalled hearing from the lips of one of my professors years ago: to be a priest means to suffer; a priest is an *alter Christus,* another Christ.

And I began in the darkness to trace the steps that led me to Tung-an. Once again I was a student at St. Joseph's school in Jasper, Indiana. Though I didn't know it then, the zealous, mission-minded Sisters were implanting in my heart the seeds of a missionary vocation. I brought my pennies to help poor Chinese children; and each Friday I took an active part in the mission day program arranged by the Sisters. I would dream dreams of telling Chinese boys and girls the wonderful story of Our Lord's life.

I recalled how the idea of becoming a priest began to crystallize when I was at Jasper Academy. But, I had told myself, the priesthood is not for me. I'm not holy enough for that, and besides I like football much better than Latin. However, Father Matthew seemed to think that one day I would be a priest; and Father Basil, our wise old Benedictine pastor, used to talk to me about the teeming millions of souls who had never heard about Our Lord, because so few went out to teach them.

At St. Meinrad's Seminary, also in Southern Indiana, especially during our mission meetings and mission plays, my thoughts often wandered to the mission fields of China. I became restless when a fellow student, Clarence Witte, went off to Maryknoll, and later my imagination flamed to the spirited words of Father Patrick Byrne (who was to become the Apostolic Delegate to Korea) when he spoke to us about Maryknoll and its mission work.

It was Bishop Byrne who gave me the vision of Christians in the world, not as mere custodians of a culture and a tradition, but as builders of something for the future, as messengers of the Eternal Word. It was Bishop Byrne who made me put this question to myself: How are you going to pay for all the blessings God has given to you? Vaguely I answered: In service to those who have not the things that I have. I remembered how with trepidation I transferred to Maryknoll, during my course in theology, with the blessing of my ordinary, Bishop Joseph Ritter, now archbishop of St. Louis. Father Basil had confidence that I could learn the language of the Orientals and that I would be happy as a missioner....

It was quiet outside and my mind kept travelling down the corridor of the years....

I was at peaceful Bedford again—our Maryknoll Novitiate in Massachusetts. I recalled, with a smile, the talks we had received on patience and humility, never dreaming that one day I would have my patience so sorely tried and my pride so painfully tested. I thought of the many books I had read about the martyrs and saintly missioners. They had seemed like men and women from a different world; heroes, only to be admired and applauded and prayed to....

How impatient I was of the long seminary course! I wanted to "get going" on my life's work among the pagans of the Orient. At last in June of 1937 I received my exciting assignment to the newly formed Maryknoll mission of Kweilin in Kwangsi Province of South China.

I recalled my family and friends coming to see me ordained. How sad they were when I departed for China. But the sorrow in my heart was outweighed by the excitement and expectancy that overwhelmed me.

Britain's over-crowded crown colony on the hilly island of Hong-Kong, with its busy arcaded sidewalks, was far too western and modern to satisfy my imagination. Happily, almost immediately, I was able to accompany Monsignor Romaniello, my superior, into the interior. The boat ride up the West River to Wuchow was more suggestive of the China of my dreams. The crude motorboat chugging desperately against the strong current barely moved forward. Lying on the floor of the frail, crowded craft was like trying to get comfortable on a large automatic drill, and the noise was just as deafening.

Chinese boys, stepping over sleeping passengers, carried steaming rice, prepared from the river water, and boiling river water tea and basins of warm water for washing. It seemed then that I would never become accustomed to the taste of food prepared that way. How I yearned for the "gift of tongues" as I watched and listened to Monsignor Romaniello laugh and talk with our smiling, carefree fellow passengers. They looked at me as much as to ask: What is the trouble with this man that he cannot speak?

I recalled my first sampan ride. This was "Old China," careless of the hours, prodigal of her children's strength, unmindful of the world's mad advance. In complete leisure I admired the beauty of the river, festive with blue lotus blossoms, and the distant hills, restful and mysterious, rising above the gently waving ocean of growing rice.

How thrilled I was when Monsignor Romaniello led me through the streets of the ancient city of Kweilin, which was to be my home for eight years. Only a handful of the thousands of people we passed were Christians, and I felt a sense of futility when faced with the overwhelming task of winning them to

Christ. There in the quiet darkness of my prison room I recalled those busy years of intense mission activity which followed the arduous months of learning the language. Then the war years: The bombings, the teeming thousands of helpless refugees, and my feeble efforts to assist them, with the generous help of the G.I.'s in Kweilin. Then the bombing of our mission church and the long flight from Kweilin after its capture by the Japanese. From then on, I was in the remote Southwest acting as chaplain with the U.S. Air Force in the Kunming-Burma area. Those years seemed centuries past.

That sleepless night, I recalled how excited I was at war's end, when, through the combined dispositions of God and my superiors, I arrived in the market town of Tung-an as its new pastor.

The mission compound, with its chapel, rectory, convent and dispensary, had been built of local gray brick by one of our older Maryknoll missioners, Father Arthur Lacroix. Just before my arrival, two new missions had been cut off from the original Tung-an territory; but still there were twenty-one mission stations for me to take care of, some as far away as thirty miles.

Once a month we would try to visit the Christians in these villages, many of which I could reach by bicycle, the others in the mountains could be visited only after day-long climbing over rough paths. But my life was in the villages which are the heart of China, where Our Lord has "much people."

It all came back to me as I lay there in the darkness—how I fell in love immediately with the rough, ancient beauty of Tung-an and the whole valley, so fortunately located geographically. It was just what I wanted, just as I had dreamed it would be. It was untouched by the penetration of modern influences, no electricity, no running water. While the livelihood of the villagers was a precarious one, by American standards, still they were economically self-sufficient. They were spared the evil of marauding bandits and marauding officials.

I was a soldier on the periphery of Our Lord's Kingdom, at one of the far flung outposts, confident that God would be with me when I was doing God's work. I was a part of the whole forward movement of the advancing Church. We would go slowly, we used to say, for China never hurries, and neither does the Church.

We would wipe out superstitions gradually. Education and hygiene would be improved; I would do my best to contribute to that. Though the genial people were poor, I would try to improve their outmoded methods of farming; though their streets were filthy and their homes dark and dirty and overcrowded, I would teach them the relationship between dirt and disease, between mosquitoes and malaria.

It was strange, that night, how only the bright spots of my life in Tung-an came to my mind. I did not recall the heartaches, the disillusions nor the disappointments. I thought of the shouting, happy youngsters flocking to the mission after school hours to play on our adobe-surfaced basketball court. I loved to watch them, and play with them and take them aside in the chapel and tell them Bible stories about Our Lord. I recalled the consolation of baptizing my new converts—one hundred and fifty adults in one year, brought in through the zeal of our Christian men and women. What high hopes I had had that one day all of the Tung-an valley would be Christian.

I was about to review the many plans we had for the future, when suddenly the stillness of the night was broken by the sound of shoes climbing the stairs; a flashlight shone in my face, I was back in my rectory prison room again.

About this time Father Frank Kelleher was passing through Tung-an. The Communist authorities ordered him to proceed under guard to Kweilin, and from there he would be escorted to the coast. Father Kelleher managed a few minutes with us, during which time he handed me a cablegram he had picked up in Ping-lo, our county seat. It read: FATHER GREENE'S MOTHER DIED SUDDENLY. PRAYERS AND SYMPATHY. BISHOP LANE.

I swallowed once or twice. It hit me very hard, but without thinking, I heard my voice saying: "In one way I'm glad; I don't think my mother could have taken this—my being here like this. God be good to her."

I remember how A-Hiu, our cook, wept when he learned the sad news. He and the Sisters spread the word among the Christians near the market and there was a large group in for my mother's Requiem Mass the next morning.

Two days after the Requiem Mass Father Nugent said to me: "Father Bob, I realize you don't want to think about this, but I was wondering if any Communist soldiers or officials offered a word of sympathy to you on the loss of your mother."

I had to admit that not one had, even though the notice had been published by the catechist on the mission gate. The ancient, tender, sensitive relationship between a mother and her son had apparently been washed from these Red brains. It would have no part in the new China, I could see. It might be a reminder of the "soft, weak" Middle Kingdom. Apparently only one's devotion to the Communist Cause was now sacred.

During this long hot summer of 1950, the first summer of Communist rule in Tung-an, we tried to plan our work as though everything would soon be normal. We had a group of prospective converts come daily to the mission for instructions. The catechumens were searched each morning as they passed by the Communist sentries at the gate, and they were ridiculed each day for coming, but they remained faithful nevertheless.

Our opportunities to spread the Faith were very great at this time; those who had hesitated during the few years prior to the change in government now started to come for instruction. They seemed to be convinced that the words "Freedom of Religion" meant just what they said. We had several village catechumenates in progress during this summer. And from letters we received from our fellow missioners we learned that prospects were encouraging all over Southwest China.

Back in 1948 we had formed the Legion of Mary in our Tung-an mission and these zealous Christians, under the banner of Our Lady, were greatly responsible for the new life that came to our mission. They would encourage the wavering, pray with the dying, and bring in prospective converts. We had three praesidia (as the Legion groups are called) in Tung-an: one for young people, and two for the older Christians. Through the summer of 1950 we were still able to hold our Legion meetings, though the Reds frowned on any type of gathering that was not Communistic—and for some diabolical reason they were most insistent on preventing the members of the Legion from meeting.

How proud we were of these apostolic Christian leaders in our Tung-an Legion of Mary. There was Tong Ta Sao, intrepid leader of the women's praesidium. She would carry out her assignments with contagious joy, and with tireless energy. Many a wayward Christian she led back to the true path, many a dying infant received from her hands the saving waters.

Another was scholarly Lin Tse-Pei, seventy-year-old president of the men's praesidium of the Legion. Years before, Mr. Lin had been a Protestant minister in the county seat. Through his reading of occidental history and long hours of prayer he finally decided to enter the Catholic Church. (The doctrine that most attracted him, he confided in me later on, was the Church's doctrine of Purgatory.)

His wide learning was admired by all, and his reputation for honesty and charity was acknowledged everywhere. A sick Christian could always expect a visit from Mr. Lin. Lax Christians knew that sooner or later he would be calling around to remind them of their obligations. His venerable, gentle manner always brought good results. When the Reds first came in he encouraged the Christians to continue to attend Mass and to continue their family prayers at home.

His scholarly talks to groups of pagans, his example of apostolic zeal, his great love for the Blessed Virgin, made him a perfect Legionnaire. How he would burn with fervor when he spoke of Our Lady: "She is our mother," he would say, "and the mother of all mankind; she will bring forth Christ again in China."

And so, should our dreams of future expansion prove premature, or even our present activities be stifled for a time, we reminded ourselves that we would have the Legionnaires of Mary carrying on Catholic Action among the people of Tung-an. They would take care of dying infants and faltering adults, they would see that prayers were said and charity practiced.

It seems stupid perhaps to say it, but we were laboring under the false premise that the restrictions imposed upon us were a "local phenomenon." We felt certain that shortly new regulations would be forthcoming "from higher up," and the absurd local situation would be straightened out. The restrictions imposed by the new regime might be warranted by the unusually strong guerrilla opposition in our area. We knew that the people at this time were opposed to the Communist oppression. And we repeated a local proverb: *A house established by oppression cannot long endure.* And we would softly discuss among the four of us, the three missioners and A-Hiu, our cook, the possibilities of the guerrillas eventually driving the Reds out of Tung-an.

Through the lowering clouds of oppression there still were streaks of reflected sunshine. We would think of the little group of catechumens preparing for Baptism in the chapel. We would continue with enthusiasm to take care of the increasing number of patients in the dispensary—even Red soldiers were there, waiting every morning for treatment. Actually many of these soldiers, wounded by the Kwangsi guerrillas, had no other means of relief, for medical men and medicine are rarities in any Chinese army.

We experienced a vague feeling of security treating the soldiers every day. A Red army medical corps officer would stand by incompetently as I washed out a bullet wound, or dug out a piece of shell. Once or twice the wounds seemed far beyond my medical knowledge, and I would explain the hopelessness of the case to the officer. He would insist that I do what I could. So after injecting a shot of morphine into the soldier I would do the best I could for the injury. My unexpressed thought each day was, What if one of these men dies while I am treating him, or dies shortly afterward? Would they possibly attach any blame to my attempt to heal him?

During these early weeks of the occupation I often met, on mission trips, some of the soldiers I treated in the dispensary. If no officer were around he would smile and greet me. But I could never understand why it was that a soldier pretended not to know me when a superior officer was standing near.

The poor peasants were always grateful for whatever we did for them in the dispensary, whether we pulled an aching tooth, or relieved a worm-infested stomach, or gave cod-liver oil to the children, or vitamin tablets to undernourished adults. Always they would bow with clasped hands on their chests and express their genuine thanks. Sometimes I'd give a glass of powdered milk to sick soldiers and children. And each day as I returned from my dispensary, tired but contented, I would think, They may continue to restrict our external activity, but there is no way of closing the dispensary—the people would never stand for that. "Even the soldiers depend too much on us for medicine to deny us this privilege of tending the people's ailments," I assured the other Fathers.

The dispensary was a much-needed outlet for the pent-up zeal of the two young Maryknoll missioners, Fathers Nugent and Gilmartin, who had arrived in Tung-an shortly before the Reds took over, to help me and to perfect their knowledge of the language. Both of them loved the people and they had acquired a considerable skill in diagnosing and treating the ailments of the hundreds of patients that came each week for relief.

It broke their hearts the morning a Communist officer came in to our quarters and ordered them to pack their things immediately and get ready to leave. "Both of you are to be deported from the country," he said curtly; then, pointing to me: "This man will remain for the time being."

It was obvious the two young priests did not want to leave, nor did they want to leave me behind alone. I tried to reassure them: "It will be only a matter of a few days before I follow you." Actually there was no way I had of knowing how long they would detain me; but somehow I was relieved to have the two Fathers spared the anxiety and the uncertainty and the torments of our house arrest. Still, saying goodbye to them was very difficult indeed.

Now that the two other Fathers had departed, Ah-Hiu would come often into the dispensary and take the opportunity to say a few words of doctrine to the people. I used to smile to hear him trying to impress the soldiers about my knowledge of medicine. He often told them of difficult cases we had handled successfully, and he reminded them of the great distances patients would travel to get medical aid from us.

Ah-Hiu never missed a chance to praise and defend us before the Communist soldiers, just as he never missed an opportunity to laud and uphold us before the pagans. I cautioned him to watch his remarks and to be less aggressive in rebuking the Communist soldiers should they speak ill of us.

But somehow the Reds seemed to respect Ah-Hiu. There was no question about it, he had an attractive personality and they seemed to enjoy talking with him. The children all over our sprawled-out mission territory knew and loved him. We would hear them cry out his name whenever we approached a distant village for a visitation.

"Ai Ya! Ah-Hiu is coming. Do some tricks for us, Ah-Hiu."

"Ah-Hiu," they'd shout, "have you any new magic?"

Even the older people would sit by the hour watching his clever acrobatics and shadowboxing performances. And many a pagan who came to marvel at Ah-Hiu's magic remained to listen to the greater marvel of Ah-Hiu's exposition of the doctrine.

Ah-Hiu came from a Christian village about four miles from the mission. His mother was an energetic, wrinkled up, pipe-smoking little woman who always reminded me of Mammie Yokum of Dogpatch, U.S.A.

She was a fervent Christian, and for miles around everyone knew clearly that Ah-Hiu's mother was a Catholic. Her large family of sons was brought up well to fear God and do justly toward their fellow man.

We would see Ah-Hiu late at night studying the meaning of the prayers or reading the Bible or the lives of the Saints. Although he had only a grammar school education, he made up in native intelligence what he lacked in formal learning. And we knew he had offers of more lucrative employment but preferred his humble work with us.

The doctrine he absorbed at night he would spread at every opportunity during the day—in the market place, in teahouses, about the dispensary. In fact we often said that he was far better at propounding the doctrine than some of the catechists, and Fathers Gilmartin and Nugent would prefer the affable and fearless Ah-Hiu as a mission-trip companion to any of our catechists.

But it was Ah-Hiu's loyalty that impressed us most. Although we had been conscious of it long before the Reds came, it was during the months after their arrival that he demonstrated almost hourly his devotion to us; and our admiration of him increased every day.

I could overhear his conversations in the kitchen directly under my room in the rectory. Communist soldiers would ask: "Why are you, a Chinese, working and slaving for these foreigners?"

"I'm not slaving for foreigners, I'm working to earn my living," Ah-Hiu would answer.

"Do you realize that when the fields of Tung-an are divided you will not receive a share unless you leave here and go to your village and produce something for the People's Government?"

"God will take care of me," confidently concluded Ah-Hiu.

"How much does the priest pay you each month?"

"I get my home here and I get enough to take care of my wife and little daughter," he said.

"But you should get more than that," they would tell him.

"I understand the People's Government insists that one is not supposed to make money," he would say. "I have enough for food and clothing, and I have some small fields that my wife cultivates. The Fathers treat me well here, and I am satisfied."

"But you are not working for the People's Government. You work for a foreign religion, and you help to spread this imperialist doctrine."

"Hold on, Comrade," Ah-Hiu said, seizing the chance to enlighten his interrogators, "the Catholic religion is not American. Its Founder was born in Palestine, and it has spread out into every country of the world. Many of our Christian leaders are native Chinese. There are twenty-eight Chinese bishops and over 2,500 Chinese priests who rule over the Church in large areas of China. The foreign priests merely establish the Church in China, and then turn it over to native Chinese priests to govern." Then he would add: "You yourself must know that the priests and Sisters have done harm to no one. They go about, as everyone understands, helping our people and teaching us to do good."

And so it would go, day after day. Ah-Hiu was proving himself to be a stalwart defender of the Faith and he never seemed happier than when he was upholding Our Lord and His Church.

He became my daily newspaper, also. Whatever gossip he picked up in the market he would give me on his return. Sometimes the news was not very pleasant, as when he excitedly reported one day a remark he had heard in a shop: "The Major says there is a noose around the Church in Tung-an, and it will soon be drawn tighter and tighter." Another day he told me that a Red officer suggested that I should turn over the mission property to the People's Government, since I would soon be expelled from China. Ah-Hiu looked at me with a plea in his eyes: "But you won't leave Tung-an, will you, Father?" He was obviously happy when I told him that I never would of my own free will.

One day, before our visits to the outlying villages were forbidden, Ah-Hiu pleaded with me not to go to a certain village high in the western mountains. "The guerrillas may kill you," he said, "to show America that there is no order in Communist China. They may hope the Reds would be blamed for your death and so provoke a war between America and Communist China because of you." Ah-Hiu had obviously forgotten that the days of "Gunboat Christianity" were over, and that my death by guerrillas *or* Communists would make small stir in Washington.

"Going to such a village is too dangerous at this time, Father," he insisted.

I said, "Well, all right, you stay here. I'll go alone. The Christians are waiting for Mass and the Sacraments. It is many months since we have been there."

Ashamed, Ah-Hiu looked down at the ground and said: "I'm sorry, Father. You are right, we'd better go."

Loyalty was the word for Ah-Hiu. We called him Gibraltar. And we were sure that he would never cause us concern. When the officials finally and irrevocably ordered him away from the mission to his home village it made me feel more alone than I had ever felt in my life. He promised to come back as soon as possible; he promised that he would watch over the Christians in his village; he promised that he would never become a Communist, come what might.

How little did Ah-Hiu (or I) know at that time the relentless, ruthless force of the Red grindstone.

CHAPTER THREE

Sister Theresa

ONE DULL DAY in October 1950, a Communist soldier rushed up to my quarters and excitedly said: "One of our officers living in town has accidentally shot himself in the leg, and he wants you to come immediately to treat the wound."

"But, Comrade, I am not permitted to leave the church property," I replied.

"We have no medical supplies, and the officer will assume all responsibility," he said.

"If you will get permission for me from the officer here, I shall be glad to go."

He secured the necessary pass and I rushed off with him and removed the bullet from the officer's leg, while in the next room a propaganda lecturer was berating the American imperialists. The Red officer's pain was obviously relieved, but no word of thanks passed his lips as he dismissed me. He would show no signs of sentimentality, at least not in the presence of the soldiers standing around.

As I came out of the officer's quarters and began unescorted to return to the mission, old Grandmother Nian's son approached me. I did not expect him to address me, but there was a plea in his eyes as he anxiously whispered: "Father, you've got to come—my mother is dying, and she cries continually for the priest to come to her before she faces God."

I knew that the pious old lady was ill; for many months she had been suffering from a cancer on her breast. Now it was critical, and it was, I realized, the end.

"Do you not know that I am forbidden to leave our quarters or to visit the homes of our Christians? It is impossible for me to see your mother without permission. It would be dangerous for all of you."

"But what can we do?" he asked hopelessly.

"Go, ask permission for me to visit your sick mother—to bring medicine for her. Don't mention the Sacraments," I cautioned him.

"And if they refuse?" he asked.

"If they refuse," I said, "you must help your mother to prepare to meet Our Lord. Make a fervent act of contrition with her, and say the rosary with her. I will pray for her at the mission."

I shall not soon forget the expression on his sad face when he returned with the verdict from the officer in charge.

"The officer said no and he gave no reason, except to say that the foreigner is not allowed to leave his quarters."

I heard the young man hopelessly pleading with the sentries for me to be allowed to visit his dying mother—but it was wasted breath. They were utterly unmoved. And what would they dare to do once the officer said no?

All that day and night I thought of Grandmother Nian lying on her deathbed outside her room—and I knew she was waiting for the priest to bring here the comforts of the Last Sacraments. I asked myself: "Will she understand, will she make her final peace with God well? Will she pray to Our Lady at the hour of death?" Somehow I was sure she would. She had lived a good Christian life and had set a fine example.

God be with her in her last agony, I prayed.

Five days later, as I was gazing out the window one morning, I saw the familiar sight of two gravediggers carrying a boxlike coffin on their shoulders and heading toward the mission from the town. As they turned off the road a short distance from the mission I saw the sad, drooping figures of Grandmother Nian's family trailing the coffin.

The traditional firecrackers were absent—this had been declared a foolish waste of money in new Red China. And I heard there was no banquet or mourning ceremony in the Nian home. Grandmother Nian died late the night before she was buried. I was sick at heart for several days, because I had wanted so much to be with this good woman when she died.

I began to ask myself: "Do the Communists mean gradually to restrict all our movements? Is there to be an end to our work for the people?" They had made no formal statement. But if I were unable to leave my room, it would mean no Sacraments for my people—a land desolate of grace.

Then I would remind myself that actually the officials had said it was for our safety that we were not permitted out. Because of guerrilla activity, it was dangerous for us. "In two or three days, perhaps, conditions will be such that you will be able to go where you choose." Always they said "in two or three days." Week after week, "in two or three days."

I rose early on the Feast of Christ the King. I was waiting in the chapel for the Christians to come for Mass, and I was surprised that none appeared. Suddenly the catechist rushed in and excitedly whispered: "The guards—they won't allow the Christians to enter the mission gate."

As I walked from the church toward the main gate, I heard a large group of Christians outside arguing with the sentries.

"But why are we not permitted to go to Church? Don't you see the sign painted by the officials on the mission wall, 'Freedom of Religion'?"

The guards repeated their answer: "You are not allowed to attend meetings here." And at the point of the bayonet they drove our good Christians away.

I knew that for several months previous to this the sentries at the mission gate had been searching the Christians for guns and messages as they entered to attend Mass. The soldiers would ridicule them and curse them, taunt them for their belief in the superstitious ceremonies of the imperialists. They had forced the Christians to register their names, addresses and occupations. Still, despite this obvious disapproval by the Communist authorities, the Christians continued to come to Mass. And it made my heart burst with pride in them to know that they would come anyway.

Actually, as I have already mentioned, during the summer of 1950, six months after the Reds took over in our area, we conducted a small catechumenate at the mission. A group of about thirty-six adults came each morning for instruction. And each day the brave, faithful catechumens would endure the jeering questions of the guards: "Why do you wish to become a Christian?"

"We wish to worship God," they would answer simply.

"What sort of thing is God?" they would ask.

"He is the great Creator about whom we are learning."

"But you should return to your village and produce something for your country instead of wasting your time here with this foreign religion."

The Red soldiers would come into the church during the doctrine classes and taunt the catechists, or ridicule the doctrine.

One day an officer entered and pointed to the altar and to the crucifix and the Tabernacle. He said he had visited many places throughout the great country of China—but never had he *seen* God. No doubt this had some effect on these simple people, but still they continued to come and thirty-four of them persevered in their study until Baptism, and their faces glowed with pride and happiness as I poured the saving water.

On this Feast of Christ the King it was the point of a bayonet that spoke; and it made me very angry to see the guards driving off the Christians. It made me very sad, too, for I knew that many of the Christians with eager steps had walked several miles to hear Mass, and now slowly they turned back to their homes with sorrow in their hearts.

I immediately went to the officer in charge.

"Why have the Christians been forbidden to enter the mission?" I asked.

"The people did not wish to enter, that is why they went away," was his illogical answer.

"Did not wish to enter?" I repeated angrily. "Why then did they come to the gate? Why did the guards drive them away with bayonets?"

"The people have begun to realize that your religion is a foreign superstition and so they did not wish to come to your meetings."

"But they *did* come—where is the logic in what you say? And how can you reconcile this unreasonable action with the Freedom of Religion sign you painted on the mission wall?"

He answered, "Freedom of religion means that you have freedom to practice your religion here. The people also have freedom of religion; but they have not the right of assembly. And furthermore no religion should take the people from their work. The Chinese people—all of them—must be productive citizens of the State."

When I made an effort to reply in defense of the productivity of the Christians, I was cursed and told that my "brain needed a washing." The officer turned angrily and left me.

The day after the Feast of Christ the King another link with my people was broken.

For fifty miles around Tung-an there was no hospital—ours was the only medical clinic—and on market day in normal times we would have between ninety and a hundred patients, some coming from villages as far as thirty miles away. The three Chinese Sisters and Father Nugent and Father Gilmartin all lent a hand at different times.

It was our only hope of continued contact with the people. They needed us, or so we thought. But the day after the Christians were driven from the mission gate on the Feast of Christ the King, the Red officials ordered our dispensary closed. They saw something else in our charity toward the people. To them it was a danger. They would find it too difficult to demonstrate the evils of imperialism and Christianity if we continued to help the people in their troubles.

When the people came with their ills, the guards told them that the foreigner had himself closed the dispensary, that he was no longer interested in their sufferings, that he refused to help them any longer. The guards went on to explain that it was well that he did close the clinic, because in other cities much harm had come to the Chinese people from these foreign dispensaries. "Many Chinese," they explained, "have been poisoned with drugs, and Chinese children have been put to death in the foreign orphanages. So, in order to protect the people of Tung-an, the dispensary would have had to be closed even if the foreigner had not closed it himself."

How many of these poor people believed this I shall never know. It was hard for me to imagine that any of them would accept the preposterous explanation after all the years of service we rendered them in their sufferings. However, as I watched and listened from inside the mission gate, I could see that the plan was subtle enough and cleverly enough presented to impress a number of these simple country folk. They were too weary and too unlettered and too fearful to demand evidence. The sly, insinuating remarks of the guards seemed to have achieved their purpose.

It was sad for me to look out at the people that morning. Some were shivering with malaria, many with their ulcerous sores, two or three with faces swollen by infected teeth. There were several mothers holding their sick and crying little ones. They would look incredulously at the guards for a bit, then they would helplessly shake their heads in bitter disappointment and slowly walk away, muttering, "Where shall we go now for medicine? There is no one who will care for our ills." The relief for which they had walked so far was denied them.

We never opened our dispensary again. I never lanced another boil, nor injected precious penicillin; I never again brought down a fever nor warmed the chill of a malaria victim with atabrine. What medicine and medical supplies we had were then "borrowed" by the officials. Since we would need the medicine no longer in the dispensary, they somehow convinced themselves that they should put it to use for the Red army.

Sad as it was to see bayonets blocking the Christians' entrance to the mission for Mass, and bitter as it was to have the door of the dispensary locked and sealed, and the sick sent away unhealed, still sadder and still more bitter was it to watch the progress of their plan to discredit me and take over for their nefarious needs the entire mission property.

Our chapel was the next target for their evil designs.

One morning as I looked out of the window toward the chapel my heart sank to a new low when I saw our main altar and the two small side altars being carried out into the yard on the shoulders of the Communist guards. Then one by one the benches were carried out. Later that day, when I was allowed out to get some water, I looked inside Tung-an's House of God. Where once had hung the crucifix and the pictures of Our Lady and the Sacred Heart, now hung a large picture of Mao Tse-tung, flanked by pictures of Stalin and other high-ranking Communist officials. The floor was covered with mud and spittle. Political signs and Communist slogans covered the walls. The desecration was complete.

After a few weeks of use as an indoctrination hall our church eventually became the first prison in the history of Tung-an, the town of "Mutual Peace." Captured guerrillas, farmers under suspicion, former officials of the Nationalist government—any leader who did not readily change—all were thrown into the chapel. Each prisoner was allotted space on the floor sufficient only to lie down.

All these soldiers and prisoners living on the mission property, and the cursing and the groaning, the singing of Communist songs, made me very anxious for the three Chinese Sisters in their convent on the other side of the church. How long would it be before *they* would be driven out?

I didn't have long to wait.

Working with us at the mission of Tung-an were Sisters Joan, Theresa, and Louise, all members of the Catechist Sisters of the Blessed Virgin. They were capable, pious, zealous nuns. In their gray habits, not unlike those worn by the Maryknoll Sisters, they were deeply respected and loved by the people. Our Maryknoll Sisters trained and directed these Chinese Sisters well during their novitiate at our diocesan see city of Kweilin ninety miles away. They were prepared for the direct apostolate. Their task was to carry Christ's message by word of mouth to the women and children.

They would spend some time each week in the dispensary, and they had become efficient at diagnosing and caring for the ills of the people. In this way they had made many friends for Christ.

Dynamic Sister Theresa, the capable leader of the little band, was a worthy daughter of her saintly and illustrious namesake. She also directed the work of the women's praesidium of the Legion of Mary.

Sometimes the Chinese Sisters with their catechists would accompany us on mission trips to distant villages. They would instruct the children and encourage the women. They would direct the Sunday school, visit the homes of the sick, call at the doors of pagans to tell them about Our Lord. They never ceased working, every hour every day riding off on their bicycles, or walking over the hills, or kneeling before the Blessed Sacrament in the chapel. Their quiet, gentle manner, their genuine interest in the problems of each family, their charity and understanding, made them revered by everyone in the Tung-an area. Even the Red soldiers appreciate their earnest devotion. Several times I saw soldiers looking over the shoulders of the Sisters as they read their prayers in the chapel.

Never did I see the patient nuns manifest any sign of distraction or annoyance.

As we had feared it would, the heavy hammer of Communism finally fell upon the Chinese nuns; the cruel Communist sickle cut from under them their feet of mercy.

The convent was "needed" for a military headquarters. The Reds sent home the women catechists, and the Sisters were ordered to go back to their native villages. But they told the officials that they could not do this. "Our place is with the people of Tung-an," they said.

However, they were expelled from their home, and managed to find a haven with a Christian family in the market. It required great faith and deep charity to welcome the oppressed nuns into this home. And the anxiety we had for these Christians was justified when we learned a few days later that the father of the family had been arrested on a trumped-up charge of subversive activities. The poor man was never heard of after that.

The Sisters moved from this home to that of another Christian family, the head of which had already been consigned to the newly created prison in our chapel. The movements of the nuns were constantly watched, the people were warned not be seen with them. The officials called them and their cook daily for questioning. Under this constant barrage of interrogations their cook's nerves gave way and she lost her mind.

The Sisters who, like us, thought that the conditions of these months were temporary begged the officials to allow them to return to the mission property. This permission was finally granted, and with hearts filled with joy, they moved into the storage room under our quarters in the rectory. Now, at least occasionally, they would be able to attend the pre-dawn Mass in our quarters, and they could suffer and pray for the speedy return of religious freedom to Tung-an.

It was obvious that the Communists wanted very much to enlist the services of the Sisters in their propaganda efforts among the women. By endless questionings, stepped up to an unbearable tempo, they tried to wear down the nuns. As I listened from the room above, it grieved me to hear the officers and the propaganda agents working on the nerves of these good women. They stood up nobly under the ordeal, and I felt my heart leap with pride at their courageous answers.

In these moments it was tiny Sister Theresa who became the spokesman for the three.

"We wish you to take over positions of authority in the Party and instruct the women." Officer after officer would thus attempt to lure them.

As always in the beginning, the Red indoctrinators would try to be proper and dignified, but when opposed they would lose their patience and composure—for anger is fatal to dignity.

Sister Theresa would stoutly reply, "That is one thing we can never do."

It was the ring of confidence, of cheerful courage, in Sister Theresa's voice that was contagious. I felt more hopeful, more confident myself. I smiled when I heard Communist Youth Corps members attempting to convert the Sisters to the Red party—though I also admired the zeal of the students. The religious habit which the Sisters loved dearly was often the bait of Red abuse. They refused, however, to remove the crucifix from their habit, or to alter the habit in any way.

But when the order came giving them three days to change their American imperialistic garb for the clothing of Chinese peasant women, there was nothing left to do but comply. They could buy nothing but white cotton cloth, and their ingenuity manifested itself when they used the carbon inside of some old flashlight batteries to dye the material almost black. It broke their hearts to make the change, but they felt that it would be for only a short while.

It was at an outdoor meeting of the Communist Ladies Auxiliary held on the mission property that Sister Theresa really showed her mettle. And I listened with rapt attention to the thrilling encounter unfold under our west window.

The officer in charge, in order to flatter the Sisters, spoke softly to them at first: "You are well-educated and refined women. You should not disgrace yourselves by being 'running dogs' of these foreigners."

Sister Theresa just as softly responded: "But we are not 'running dogs' of any foreigners; we are nuns of the Catholic Church."

"You are working for foreigners, are you not?"

"No, we are working for God."

"But why are you not working for your country? Your country needs women like you."

Firmly and calmly Sister Theresa replied: "Whom do we treat in the dispensary? To whom do we give medicine? Are these sick not our own people? And whom do we teach to be obedient children of their parents and honest, loyal citizens of our country? Are they not Chinese children?"

The officer, losing face as well as patience, angrily shouted: "You teach Chinese to be obedient to this foreign priest."

"That is not true," said Sister Theresa. "We teach the people to obey God, and to comply with the legitimate laws of the People's Government."

"But what do you teach?" he snapped.

"Just that," replied the frail nun. "Just what I have told you. The people have heard our teaching in the open. We have never taught in secret. We teach them to be good, to love God, and to be good citizens of China."

Theresa's calm firmness seemed to disturb this man more than the cool logic of her speech. But he wouldn't give up, he greedily returned to the familiar taunts.

"You nuns do not marry. Why are you forbidden to marry?"

"Comrade, do you not tell the young members of the Communist Party that *they* should not marry? Your soldiers have told me that they are to give themselves, at least for several years, fully and wholeheartedly to the work of the Communist Party."

"That is quite different."

"No, that is quite the same. Our reason is the same, except that we consecrate ourselves to God, and we do it for life."

"You are very clever," he sneered. "The foreigners have educated you well."

"No, Comrade," replied Theresa with tantalizing calmness. "We are not clever. We know only the simple truths of God's religion."

"You are educated. You can read and write," he said, "and few women can do as much. You have had much experience teaching and you are able to influence the women and children. Why do you not enter the service of the People's Government and teach the doctrine of Communism?"

"Thank you, Comrade, but we have no abilities but to teach the catechism. We know only the religion of the Catholic Church. We have no experience in other matters."

"But you could learn. With your ability you would go far in the Communist Party."

"Perhaps we could learn, but we have already given ourselves to God."

The officer, beside himself with rage, stumped off and growled something under his breath at the nuns.

During all these endless questionings, repeated day after day, Sister Theresa never became impatient. She never appeared or sounded belligerent. She always was sure and firm and unafraid. And it did me good to hear her champion her God and her calling before these rude and ruthless men. Each time the questioning began I would start to pray for the Sisters and wish that I could take their places, though I doubted that I could stand up as well under the planned attacks.

Though there was no sign of wavering in their loyalty nor of any weakening in their resolve never to work for the Party, I could see that the secondary end of the questionings was being achieved. The Sisters had become quite nervous and ill. Even Sister Theresa eventually began to show signs of the strain the constant interrogations caused her. And I cautioned her to be careful in her answers and not to get herself or the Sisters into trouble.

"But, Father, I must tell these men the truth. I feel that it is God speaking through me at these times, for of myself I could never find answers for all their questions, nor strength and patience to endure."

Forever in my memory will be the morning these three wonderful nuns in the simple garb of peasant women came with the disheartening word that they had been ordered from the mission and told to return to their native villages immediately.

Tears streamed down their faces as they knelt to ask my blessing. My hand shook as I made the sign of the cross over them.

Sister Theresa, still kneeling, said in her clear, confident way: "We are not afraid, Father—we are fearful only that harm will come to you. You know, Spiritual Father, we will never accept

Communism. We will never deny Our Lord. They can kill us but we will be loyal."

The three Sisters rose, bowed, turned and slowly walked away. It was the last time that I saw them—though it was not the last time that I was to hear the voice of Sister Theresa.

CHAPTER FOUR

"The Maniac"

"HOUSE ARREST" is a misleading euphemism. In plain everyday language it means that your home becomes a prison, your room a prison cell. You are confined as a criminal, treated as a criminal, and feel like a criminal. The bars on your room windows are the bars of a prison cell, your room door becomes the guarded gate of a prison cell. Normally a prisoner has the satisfaction of knowing clearly that he is confined for breaking some law. In "house arrest" you are never informed why you are under constant guard, and you have the added annoyance of being reminded that you are technically "free."

As I have said, in Tung-an there was previously no prison or jail. Our mission church became the jail, and my rectory was the prison annex.

It was not the restrictions that caused me concern, nor was it the fear of physical punishment. It was the thought of my Christians living and suffering and dying without the Sacraments, and it was the planned, hour-by-hour, day-after-day, nerve-wracking annoyance of the mind that was beginning to wear me down. This psychological torment, this persecution of the mind, this water-dripping torture of the brain, this was the insidious, subtle method devised to break me. The weight was to become unbearable, and I know for certain that, but for the grace of God and the aid of the Blessed Mother, I never could have withstood it.

It was not until this ever present pressure began to gain momentum that the "master plan" became clear to me. The constant insults and indignities piled up. The hourly invasion of my privacy—actually there was no privacy—went on. I was like the main attraction on a carnival midway. This was one of the Communist "freedoms"—freedom of inspection. There is no home or room exempt from the prying eyes of these inspection teams. Groups of students or soldiers hourly break in and announce that they are holding an inspection. It seemed that my rectory room prison was the planned target for most of the inspectors and tormentors.

I might be attempting to read or say a rosary, or, as in so many cases, preparing or eating my rice. A team of about ten would come in, ask a few questions and then start through my personal possessions. A bit of my toothpaste would be squeezed out and tasted, the toothbrush fingered; razor blades were tested, in fact often the shaving equipment was taken out and used on the almost beardless faces of the young soldiers. They would thumb through the two or three books I had been allowed to keep. They would sniff and touch my food.

They would ask the meaning of the rosary they found near my bed. They would open every drawer and hold up the contents for inspection; they would try on my clothes and ridicule them and me. Pictures were examined, and each one had to be explained.

Had this been a single inspection, once only and then over

with, it would not have been so difficult to bear. But several times a day I went through the same process, the same testing, the same taunting, the same questions, the same answers. Once they entered, I prayed they would quickly depart, that they would leave me alone. Group after group, question after question, there was no relief, team followed team. They were fresh and eager, I was weary and uninterested. My patience was sorely tried. Day by day the noose was losing its slack.

Pointing to my typewriter one rustic young boy of a soldier sneered: "We all know that you are a spy for the imperialistic Americans—this machine is proof. With this we know that you send out messages to Hong Kong and Japan."

I almost smiled, but it was frighteningly apparent that the lad was deadly serious. And I felt helpless as I tried to explain to him that it was used merely to write English.

The Youth Corps students were as bad. They would come in teams of ten or twenty, sometimes in mixed teams of girls and boys. But always with the same prearranged plan of inspection and questionings. Rudely kicking open the door of my room, they would enter with their muddy shoes and stand around at attention for a moment, spitting on the floor and then starting the barrage.

One common vexation was the sincere effort of these young people to convert me. Each in his turn would expound for my benefit the glories of Communism, or the glories of Mao Tse-tung or Stalin. One by one they would take up the evils of imperialism, the wrongs committed by America in Korea and in Manchuria. No longer were they asking: how high are the buildings in America? Or, how many cars are there in America? How fast can they go? Now it was: are there Communists in America? Are there always strikes in America? Why does America want to fight China?

I recall one member of the Youth Corps, a fine looking chap about twenty years of age, asking one day: "What is your attitude toward the People's Government?"

I replied: "I have no special attitude toward it. We hear that it has been established to help the people. If it does that and allows the people to worship God it is good."

"What is your salary?"

"We receive no salary," I replied.

"Then how do you live? Where do you get your money?"

"We get our means of support from the sacrifices of Catholics in America," I said. "They make it possible for us to carry on our good works here in China for the Chinese people."

At that there was laughter and the young questioner hissed: "Everyone knows that you are an agent for the United States government, and you get your money from your government."

"I am an agent of the Catholic people of America who wish to spread the religion of Jesus and to help those in need," I said.

"What of your wife and children in America?"

"We priests do not have wives; we are not permitted to marry," I explained. "We are similar to the young Communists who must devote all their time and energies to their cause."

These same interrogations were repeated day after day. I thought of writing out the answers to the questions and passing them out to each group as it came in.

"Do you eat rice? Do you like Chinese food? Is it true that you eat much meat? Is it better than American food? Why do you use knives and forks?" And on and on they went.

Occasionally the officer in charge of the military personnel occupying the mission would come in with a group of young men, and he would often turn his questions to the subject of religion. With the condescending air of a schoolteacher quizzing a dull student, he would say, "You say you worship the Lord of Heaven. Have you ever seen Him?"

And that question, as was expected, caused a ripple of laughter among the young soldiers.

I would reply: "No, I have never *seen* the Lord of Heaven, no more than I have seen my great great grandfather; nor have I seen the maker of this desk. But from the effects I do see I can reason to the cause in every case. So with the orderly universe, we know that this must have an intelligent cause. We call that cause the Lord of Heaven."

"No intelligent people believe that superstition. You should have your brain washed," he said, dismissing the answer with a wave of his hand.

Then he would speak about the "unscientific" doctrines of the Christian religion. I reminded him one day of the large number of learned scientists who believe in God. And I showed him a chart with the names of great scientists listed thereon. He gave it a casual glance and sneered: "You see, just as I thought—no Russian or Chinese scientists on this list, and they are the world's best scientists." And in this way he dismissed that argument.

I tried to explain the historic coming of Christ, but they chuckled and blasphemously ridiculed the Virgin Birth and life of Our Lord. Each group used the same slanderous words repeated parrot-fashion—words they had heard in the daily Communist indoctrination classes held on the mission property under my window.

I had been told months before by the Sisters that the students and soldiers had been instructed to do just what they were now doing: to keep bothering me, keep testing my patience, wear me down.

Repeatedly the officials came in and officiously demanded

that I fill out questionnaires, to be answered in Chinese and English—often the same set of questions several times in the same week. It may be of interest briefly to recall some of these questions, and the manner in which I responded.

Question: Where were you born?

Answer: Jasper, Indiana, U.S.A.

Question: What schools did you attend in America?

Answer: St. Joseph School, Jasper Academy, St. Meinrad Seminary, Maryknoll Seminary.

Question: What courses did you study in each school?

Answer: (Followed the long list of studies pursued in each of my schools.)

Question: When did you come to China and what places have you visited in China?

Answer: (I gave the date of my arrival in China and listed the provinces and cities I visited during almost fifteen years.)

Question: Who is the head of your Society's Far Eastern Bureau?

Answer: Maryknoll has no Far Eastern Bureau. My superior is Monsignor Romaniello of Kweilin.

Question: Do you have guns in your house or on your property?

Answer: No.

Question: To what political party do you, as a Catholic, belong in America?

Answer: I do not belong to any political party. The Church does not regulate this matter.

Question: Do you know President Truman?

Answer: Yes, just as every Chinese knows Mao Tse-tung.

Question: How many people in your family? List the occupation of each.

Answer: (I listed my deceased father and my brother and their occupations.)

Question: Do they own land?

Answer: No, they rent their property.

Question: What is your attitude toward the officials of the People's Government?

Answer: I do not know the officials of the People's Government, therefore I cannot answer.

These forms were always carefully folded and taken away, and I often thought my file of them must be enormous.

Of all the groups that came in to torment and question me it was, I thought, the teams of small children that caused me the most annoyance. They were assigned the duty of arousing the people in the early morning and of inspecting their homes.

In groups of ten or twelve, led by a youngster carrying a flag, they would march in and take their positions. Actually my heart went out to these children with their brains so obviously washed, and filled with hatred for me and for all I stood for. I could not blame them; they did not know what they were doing. And I knew that their parents no longer had any control or influence over them. Parental authority had already collapsed. Parents had become afraid of their children, for they knew that the reward was very great for the child who informed on his parents.

Some of these children I would recognize as members of Catholic families, some I would recall having treated in the dispensary; all of them I had seen around the market place of Tung-an.

I would smile a welcome at them, but my smile would be met by a stony, cold stare, with a sneer of hatred on their young faces. They would look at my room, point to something that seemed to them out of place, or to any dust or dirt that might be around.

On one occasion, in the group of children was one of my Catholic boys—God obviously had been washed from his little brain. He severely scolded me for some dirt he saw in the hallway downstairs. "It should be cleaned up," he snapped.

"The dirt downstairs was left there by the soldiers, not by me," I answered as patiently as I could.

One of the other boys said angrily: "You should not speak that way about the soldiers of the People's Government."

I ignored the lad and turned to the Catholic youngster. "Ah-San, you know that I have been many times to your home and you know also that in comparison my house is very clean."

This caused a chorus of curses from the children, and they marched out showering abusive language at me, sickening to hear from their young lips.

Evening after evening teams of youngsters would gather in the street under my window singing the Communist songs, one of which they repeated several times to serenade me: "If there were no Communist Party there would be no Great China." In the midst of their singing, stones started to fly through the window, and shouts of fiendish glee welled up from the street as they ran away. Soldiers standing nearby made no effort to interfere—rather they encouraged them. There was nothing I could do about it; I was helpless to reprimand or stop these children. There was no one to whom I could protest, or from whom I could ask protection.

During these days and months even though there was no serious physical pain (I often wished there were, so that I could offer something tangible to God), still I felt weak and sick and I would drop on my knees to pray for strength.

Then, of course, this constant confinement meant continual

physical inactivity. Previously there had been daily duties—the dispensary, sick calls, long mission trips over the mountains, teaching, preaching and visiting. Now there was only sitting and pacing my cell, wondering, waiting. It told on my nerves. It was difficult to think, difficult to console myself with the thought that it was God's will, difficult to pray, or to read. I could not refrain from wondering what form the *next* torment would take and by whom. Nor could I hold back the temptation to ask myself: why is this happening to me now? So much remained to be done for these people who were becoming so receptive to the Gospel teaching.

At first, in a humorous way, and later, oh, so seriously, I would tell myself: "This is your 'second novitiate'." And now as I look back on those weeks when I was alone I recall that they amounted to exactly fifty-two—a year's novitiate!

One of the big thorns in my side at this time was the Red army indoctrinator. He was a boisterous, thickset Major, about thirty years old and a high Party man as well. He had come occasionally when the other two Fathers were with me; now he came regularly. He told me he had been working for the Communist Party since he was twelve years old. Before their expulsion Fathers Gilmartin and Nugent had tabbed him the Maniac, because of his fanatical, diabolical zeal for Communism, and because of his uncontrollable and intense hatred for Americans and America. Wildly wielding his cane, pacing up and down in my room he would rant and rave about the inhuman treatment of Chinese prisoners of war by American soldiers in Korea. He would describe the brutal bombing of innocent Chinese across the Yalu River, and he would boast of the powers of the Chinese soldiers in comparison to the weak, timid Americans. How many times have I heard him brag: "One Red soldier is equal to twenty Americans." And he would repeat the figure for emphasis, so that the soldiers standing around in the room would take note.

Other inquisitors repelled me and annoyed me; the Maniac scared me. Sometimes I would be looking out of the window and would see him approaching the rectory, and unconsciously I would pray to be delivered from his presence.

He would burst into the room and strut up and down in front of me. Most of the time he would start quietly enough on the glories of Communism, and gradually work himself into white-heat frenzy. His eyes would flare with a venomous hatred whenever he mentioned America. He no longer seemed like a man with a mind, rather he became transformed before my eyes into something inhuman, something fiendish. He would brandish his cane in front of me, sometimes banging it on the table, sending a shudder through me. The strain and tension was terrific.

"You have guns and ammunition hidden in your house. Why do you not confess it?" This was a daily question yelled at me by the Maniac. "Just admit that you have them; that's all you are asked to do."

"Now look," I would say, "I should be glad to give you the guns if I had them, so that you would not be troubled questioning me. Why do you not have your men search the house again and see for yourself?"

"You're too clever; you've got them too well hidden." Then he added, "I've been trying to help you, but if you insist on hiding your guns, I can do nothing for you."

With some such remark as this he would abruptly walk out, leaving me utterly exhausted and limp. The ordinary unlettered soldiers and the endless teams of shallow-thinking students were relatively easy to handle and easy to endure. Nothing could be compared to the Maniac.

Oddly enough, he understood considerable Catholic doctrine.

He had heard, he said, that I told the people the Communists were "Red Devils." And just as I was trying to frame an answer to that I noticed that his angry demeanor had changed and a queer smile broke out on his face. He seemed to have accepted the epithet smugly enough—almost as though he considered it a compliment. He did not want me to answer.

It was the Maniac who first leveled his bitter tongue at Our Blessed Mother. He seemed to take a devilish delight in taunting me about the Virgin Birth and our devotion to Mary.

There was another officer who called regularly during these weeks. He was the commander of all the forces operating from the headquarters in the Sisters' convent. Every sentence falling from his lips would start with the two words: "I say," or "I'm speaking," and in his northern dialect the expression sounded not unlike the name of the Polish capital. So Father Gilmartin early named him "Major Warsaw."

Major Warsaw was a cruel, cold, stern Party officer, but his voice was rarely raised in uncontrolled anger. His technique was to pierce like a stiletto; the Maniac's normal attack was the broadsword.

For hours Major Warsaw would sit and persistently pour out for my edification his tale of the glories of Communism. He was dead serious as he attempted to wash my brain, to convert me to his way of thinking. He would try to convince me that the Christian religion was utter superstition. The reasoning of this poorly educated man was shallow to an extreme but it was difficult to argue with him.

One day he spent considerable time trying to show that man has no soul.

"In what way are we different from dogs and other animals if we do not have a soul with will and intellect?" I remember asking him.

That one time his voice did rise and he angrily yelled: "Do you mean to say that we Communists are like animals?"

"If you deny the existence of a spiritual soul I cannot see the difference."

He filled the room with muffled curses and stormed out. An hour or so later he was still fuming when he returned to berate me for my stubborn and impolite manner, and remind me that things would go hard for me unless I confessed that I had guns and that I had aided the anti-Communist forces.

My Red captors kept me "informed" of events in the outside world. Mail from the U.S. had been cut off long ago. While the Sisters were still with us and received some news, I could follow sketchily the lives of the Christians. After they were sent home, it was Major Warsaw who supplied the news. Actually I was living as in a well, seeing nothing and hearing nothing of the world outside. With great glee the Maniac would gloat about the Red victories in Korea. "America, with all its vaunted power," he would shout, "is confined to a small strip of territory in feeble Korea. You will see one day the might of the great Red armies as they sweep the imperialistic American forces into the sea."

How he revelled in his tirades against America, unable to constrain his deep hatred and utter disgust! "Don't you know that the economic structure of your filthy country is toppling over? Look at the endless breadlines, look at the strikes that cripple your production." (Oh, how many times he referred to the strikes.) "The soft easy American way—made possible by exploiting the Asiatic peoples—is at an end," he would say. As he ranted, from time to time he would glance at the soldiers crowded into my room; they seemed impressed and fascinated. I was annoyed and disgusted.

Then he would lower his voice a bit and try a feeble attempt at gentle persuasion: "Why do you want to go back to such a country? Why do you not wash your brain of superstitious and imperialistic ways and remain in this young, new, vigorous country of ours and enjoy real happiness?"

And in a confidential tone (if that were possible for him) he would stand in front of me and ask: "Do you know the size of the great Russian army? It is larger than all the imperialistic armies of the world combined. Do you understand that?

"And do you know that the greatest scientists of the world are in Russia? For example," he enlightened me, "Russian scientists have succeeded in making rain. They have no need of your Divine Providence to produce it."

His lowered voice encouraged me to explain: "I think rain has been produced artificially in America. But American scientists do not yet claim to have the power to make clouds."

Bang went the cane on the table by my side. "You imperialists are all filled with lies. You take credit for all discoveries. Only now are we learning the truth—namely, that most all scientific inventions came originally from our great friend and benefactor, Russia."

What surprised me most in the explosive tirades of the Maniac and the cold declamations of Major Warsaw was their grasp of things Christian. They knew the number of missionaries Maryknoll and other societies had in South China. They would often refer to Chinese priests who had been enrolled in the American Imperialist Spy Ring. The Maniac gloatingly greeted me one morning with the news that two reactionary Chinese priests had been executed in Hupei for carrying on anti-Communist activity.

The Maniac would growl: "It is unpatriotic for Chinese men to follow the dictates of the leader of all imperialistic activities, the Pope in Rome."

I reached for a catechism and pointed out to him that Christians are taught to be good and loyal citizens of the State. "They must obey the legitimate laws of their country, and defend their country in time of danger." The Catechism's explanation of patriotism proved unconvincing to the well-washed brain of the Maniac. Nor did the few passages of St. Paul relative to obeying authority have any effect. A smug smile might replace the angry growl—as much as to imply: "Do you expect me to believe that? We are not fooled by what you write in your lying doctrine books."

Major Warsaw found delight in taunting me about our title "Shen fou"—Spiritual Father. (The most polite names by which they now addressed me were either "Comrade" or "Old American".) The Major would sneer: "You say you have no wife or family, yet you insist on the title Spiritual Father in order proudly and arrogantly to lord it over the Chinese people. You make the Chinese people kneel down before you and try to subject their thoughts and actions to your will."

"You are wrong, Comrade," I said, "we do not ask the people to kneel to us, but to God alone. We priests are men like our people. We are addressed as Spiritual Father merely because it is a title, like your title of Major among your men. The Church is a family and the Christians are like spiritual children whom we try to lead in the way of obedience and love toward God and fellow men."

Though it sorely tried my patience and tantalizingly tested my nerves to the breaking point to be thus taunted and subjected to these daily ordeals, what I found most difficult to endure was the repetitious chanting of Mao Tse Tung's praises by Major Warsaw and the Youth Corps members. These were not cutting remarks that jabbed and stung for a moment. These were endless words enthusiastically parroted from the lips of propaganda officers and quoted from Party textbooks. I began to learn by heart the glorious history of Mao. He was a poor but honest boy who had turned his back on his unjust landowner parents. He championed the underdog, the downtrodden, and the peasant as a young man. He fought against the bandit Chiang for a free People's Government. His great mercy toward those who went astray, his unlimited ability in statesmanship, in military matters, in economics, in building bridges and roads designed and engineered by him—all were apparent. So it went on and on ad nauseam.

Then the group would sing a hymn praising the (almost) divine powers of Mao—he was their savior. I told myself that the propaganda leaders had certainly done a thorough job of presenting Mao to the Chinese people.

CHAPTER FIVE

The Red Nun

IT IS THE extraordinarily efficient organization of Communism that keeps forcing itself on one's mind—the system has been well tried, and the strategy is clear and orderly.

It was impossible not to observe the similarity between many of their "mission" methods and those which we used. It was Sister Theresa who first brought it home to me: "Father, they are using our catechumenate system of teaching the doctrine." In our instructions, prior to Baptism, we would teach the catechumens in small groups according to their mental capacities. These groups were called catechumenates.

The Reds used the same small group system of instruction. Soon after they moved into the mission property, they began to organize these groups, and train them in the Communist doctrine and history. And what grieved me most was that the instruction was taking place on our compound, right under my west window, within easy listening distance.

Ordinarily the genuine Party members conducted these catechumenates. These "missionaries," most of them from distant parts, seemed to be on fire with zeal, bursting with enthusiasm, filled with the Party line. The people were from villages surrounding Tung-an; they came, reluctantly at first, to have their minds washed of their old ideas and filled with the new doctrine of Communism. And it was impressed upon them that they were to return as apostles among their village people to spread the new hope for China and the world.

The "catechumenates" were divided into sessions for women, older men and young people. Each group received the doctrine according to its capacities to absorb it.

Classes for school children of grammar grades, provided with food by the Red government, went on daily for a month with the same youngsters in attendance. As in our own Christian doctrine classes, the indoctrinator would first shout out a question and then give the answer. The children, some of them my own Christian children, baptized by me, would repeat the words in the same singsong fashion. Some of the questions I can still hear ringing in my ears: "Who is the great liberator of China?" "The great liberator: our leader, Mao Tse Tung." "What country is the great enemy of our people?" "The imperialistic country of America." "Within our country who are the oppressors of our people?" "The landlords and capitalists." "Who is the great traitor to our country?" "Chiang Kai-shek, because he sold out our country to the imperialists." "Why are our people poor and ill fed?" "Because of the landlords, who must be abolished."

And so it went, children being fed on lies and hatred, worked up to a feverish frenzy by these songs of fanatical hate, imbued with a diabolical desire to sacrifice all for the Cause of Communism in the great new China. And my heart felt sick to see their innocent minds turned to bitterness. I felt my helplessness to stop it. They were taught that no one—parents or friends—should ever stand in the way of loyalty to the New China.

However, the main effort of the rabid indoctrinators was expended on the youth, youngsters between the ages of fourteen and twenty-five. They formed the Chinese New Democratic Youth Corps, a continuation of the Chinese Socialist Youth Corps founded back in 1920 in Shanghai. In 1928 the name had been changed to the Communist Youth Organization, and in 1946 it was given its present name. Now it is a mass organization of all groups, young farmers, students, young workers and soldiers. It demands unswerving loyalty to the Marx-Leninist cause, absolute obedience to the Government and Party leaders, and a spirit of absolute self-sacrifice. They are to be the leaven which will penetrate all the youth of China with the spirit of Communism.

They train others for public speaking; they correct erroneous tendencies inside the organization; they are the apostles carrying the message to everyone. Not only are they expected to wash their brains of all capitalistic and reactionary and conservative tendencies, they are to root out all "individual pride, individual heroism, romanticism, self-complacency, all liberalism, all feelings of class superiority."

Each village would send in its representatives, who would be made apostles to return to their neighborhood and spread the ideals of Communism and make other converts to the new regime. These young people were the zealots who manifested the deepest desire to "go out into the whole world" and preach this gospel to change the old into a new Communist dominated world. To win members for the Party is the duty and constant task of every Youth Corps.

These meetings for the youth were conducted every night, and they would go on sometimes until near midnight. They were attended not only by the students, but by young people who had already worked hard all day in the fields or in a shop.

It was drilled into their young minds that the Communist Party is fighting for the liberation of all mankind—not only for the establishment of the Party in China. Therefore, each member of the Youth Corps must dedicate himself to the Communist Cause; he must fight for it and form a revolutionary view of life which will lead to the final victory. He must study and develop a firm unwavering faith in the future of the world Communist society. He must be prepared for long, hard work and possible setbacks; he must be prepared at any moment to sacrifice his very life. The true Communist Youth must have an indomitable spirit of sacrifice and struggle. The youth of China must set a shining example for the oppressed children of the whole world, who will learn to revere them and follow in their footsteps.

These are the words I heard from my window being poured nightly into the eager ears of the young people who came to my mission to be set on fire with the new Red poison. After they were sufficiently grounded in the elementary principles they were to be sent out two by two into the poorest hovels and the most remote villages. In two weeks or so they returned to the mission property and reported on their successes and their failures. At these sessions they would listen to experienced Party Members and they would ask questions and get the answers. They were then given the program to be followed on their next mission. And they would conclude the meetings by shouting the words: "Mao Tse-tung is our Liberator—without a Communist Party there would be no China. Down forever with Imperialist America!"

As I listened to the training of these young Communist missionaries and saw their fire and zeal, I began unconsciously to realize more and more that I was witnessing the operation of an organization similar to my own Church.

This Communist "Church" certainly has "unity." There was obviously a oneness of command ("Mao ordered it. . . .it must be done"), and a oneness of doctrine (Marx, Lenin, Stalin and Mao), and a oneness of *purpose* (world Communism).

It has "universality:" no village in China is free from its influence, no country in the world is immune to its scourge. In the officers' quarters fixed up in the Sisters' convent, I saw a huge map of the world with red flags stuck into those countries already fallen into Communist hands: Poland, Latvia and the rest. Sometimes in parades I saw soldiers representing each of the Red allies of China—North Korea, East Germany, Poland and the others.

And in their plans and aims the doctrine of Communism was to be carried into every city and village of the world. It was for all mankind. All men were to be made equal; classes were to be done away with. Thus they repeated, in a new way, their ancient proverbs: "All under heaven are one family; all within the four seas are brothers."

I saw also the "apostolicity" of the Communist religion. Every true Communist must be an apostle. They are willing to leave home and family—yes, to hate father and mother—for this Cause.

I talked with young Communists in my town in Southwest China, who had come all the way from Shantung in the Northeast, from Manchuria in the far north and they put no limits on the distance they were willing to go, or the hardships they were willing to undergo. There were no hardships for them, in fact. Every difficulty, every obstacle and inconvenience was accepted as part of the program for the Cause. They were not conservative—I never met a Communist who was conservative.

No real apostle can be satisfied merely to conserve what he already has. They would talk Communism at every opportunity; they would create opportunities to talk it.

One Saturday, shortly after the Reds came into Tung-an, while the Christians were still coming to Mass, a young Communist Corporal came and demanded permission to address the people after our ceremony was over. Under the circumstances, it was impossible to refuse, even though I knew he was about to pour poison into ears that had just received the word of God.

During their free time, the soldiers walking about the market would often stop a man and start to expound the Communist line—for this they were made to understand they would receive much "kung-lao" (merit). Students after school hours would visit homes, or teach smaller children Communist songs and speeches. They were made to realize their obligation to convert anyone who had not yet understood the advantages of Communism and its glories. They were taught to report all signs of deviation from the Party line—any reactionary tendencies in their own or other villages, in their own or other families. And for any report of this nature they would be rewarded. But, for the most part, their tireless efforts and ceaseless journeyings were never rewarded with a monetary remuneration.

Once I asked a group of young men: "How much does the Party give you for working so many long hours each day?"

"What are you saying?" they asked indignantly. "It is of no consequence what we receive; we do this for our country and the Cause."

Sometimes these apostles would come in with muddy shoes and I'd say: "You have travelled far today, Comrade." Always there would be the same smile of indifference to difficulty and always: "Meh you kuon hsi"—"It is of no consequence; we are anxious to do this for the Cause." Every suggestion from me that things were difficult for them or that their life was hard was greeted with a shrug and the repeated: "Meh you kuon hsi-meh you kuon hsi. It is of no consequence. . . . it is of no consequence."

Many an hour they spent trying to indoctrinate me. I can still see one young Red who tried time and again to convert me. His eyes would glow as he went on and on: "Sooner than you can imagine Communism will be in every country on earth. The whole world will be one, it will be ours. Our great leader, Mao Tse-tung, will free us from the oppressors; the exploitations and the humiliations inflicted upon us by the imperialistic Americans will be at an end."

They never guessed how revolting to me was their constant eulogizing of Mao. In speaking of him, they would use words that we would use in referring to Our Lord—actually in some of the patriotic songs, Mao was given attributes that belong only to the Divine. The life of Mao, the speeches of Mao, the plans of Mao, were all required reading for every young Chinese. Mao was their hero and their savior.

In my mind I shall always keep Sister Theresa, the Chinese nun of Tung-an, as the noble and heroic exemplar of courageous, selfless womanhood. She was everything good, everything pure, everything kind.

But when I think of Sister Theresa, there crowds into my mind another Chinese woman of Tung-an. We gave this young zealot the nickname of "Connie Commie." Often we had remarked about the tireless zeal of Sister Theresa—here was a woman to match her. We had been held spellbound by Sister Theresa's clear enthusiastic exposition of the doctrine; here was a voice, raised in another cause, just as clear and just as enthusiastic. Sacrilegious as it may seem, I found myself referring to her often in my mind as the Red Nun.

Both Sister Theresa and Connie Commie could talk the language of the most unlettered peasant and both could talk for hours on end and both could read and write and talk with educated students and professors.

Connie Commie obviously came from a good family. She was always well-dressed and neat, and well-liked.

From my upper room window I could listen to her addressing groups of women with fiery eloquence. She could go on without a break longer than any speaker I have ever heard. Then shrewdly she would question the women on the matter covered. Although her shrill voice under my window drove me almost insane, I could not refrain from admiring her zeal and her persuasive powers. Here again was proof of the thoroughness of Communist methods and their penetration of all social strata.

She would shout out "We must change the world" to these poor peasant women who never thought of any place beyond the range to which their feet could carry them in one day. Yet somehow she could get these women excited about changing the world, and I would notice a stir among these listeners as though they really believed what Connie Commie was saying. Perhaps what appealed to the women most was Connie Commie's exposition of what Mao Tse-tung was doing for the women of China and the great part they were to play in the New China. For the first time they were spoken to about "social and economic reconstruction" about "production" and "political ideologies." They may not have understood the words but these illiterate women had a feeling of pride in being talked to about them.

Connie Commie, like Sister Theresa, had a special way with

the children. Sister Theresa would often have little candies for the youngsters. Connie Commie, too, always carried sweets for the children—bought by her own meager funds, so a soldier told me—and would ask them for information about their parents and families. She seemed so polite and sympathetic when talking with the women; obviously the women liked her and liked her interest in their children and their problems. She was always pleasantly greeted by the women as they passed her in the market place or on the road under my window.

Once she came to me for medicine: "I have some friends who are ill with malaria," she said, "and I wish to take some medicine to them."

"The government has sealed up my supplies," I replied, "and I am not free any longer to dispense medicine."

However, I gave her a few of the atabrine pills which I had in a drawer, held out when the officials closed our dispensary. As I handed her the medicine I thought: I had planned to use these pills to draw souls to Christ—now this woman will use them to draw souls to Sa. . . . no, I should not say that, for it may not be true. It may not be true that they are taking souls to Satan, but it is certainly true that they are taking my people away from Christ. Of that I have evidence.

Connie Commie began slowly to reveal the glamorous emptiness of collective life. Several times I overheard her bitterly denouncing others within the Party, narrating their faults to the officer in command. Her smiling, cheerful face would harden into a sneering expression as she would relate the evils of imperialistic America or Chiang Kai-shek. If anyone attempted to cross her or even propose a question, she would fly into a terrific rage. She could not allow any thoughts except those that agreed with the Party line, any acts but those that attained the Communist goal.

One day I overheard this tireless machine of flesh and bones addressing the women on the "backwardness of past ways," the emancipation of women in political and social life. And she spoke about former superstitions. It was at this point that I heard her raise her voice angrily as she condemned the superstitions of Christianity. And the surprising thing to me was that she could enumerate in detail so many tenets of our Christian Faith, and try to explain to the people the "falsehood" involved. I heard her say that the foreign priests deceive people, and she ridiculed the idea of God. These simple people would laugh as she asked, "Did anyone ever see the Lord of Heaven? Did anyone ever see a spirit?"

Then the practical aspects of her hours of indoctrination would wind up with Connie Commie grouping the women in cells and assigning them duties to perform in their villages. She was making apostles out of them—"Make sure," she would plead, "that there is no sign of reactionary movements in your village. We, the women of China, must unite with one heart to crush the old imperialist enemies and free the oppressed women of the world." No longer were these unlearned women mere commodities to be sold, they were part of a united revolutionary effort.

I used to marvel at the Red Nun's limitless energy, her contagious zeal, her diabolical hatred for Christianity, her persuasive personality, and I would often ask myself: what reward was this young woman receiving for her tireless efforts? It could not be to satisfy her vanity; and it was not, I knew, for money. I got my answer one day when I saw the exuberant expression on her face and learned that the reason for her great joy was that she had at last been accepted as a "full-fledged member" of the Communist Party. That, I mused, is her goal—the Party.

While among the Chinese Communists in our Tung-an area there were a few outstanding individuals like Connie Commie, most of the work of organization and indoctrination was carried on by small well-knit units or "cells". Not until after the Reds came did I learn that cells were operating in Tung-an long before the army arrived. Each cell consisted of about ten or twelve members. In the army the cell was a squad led by a corporal who ordinarily was a full-fledged Party member. The lay propaganda teams were also composed of about ten or twelve young people under a Youth Corps leader.

From my window I could see them come into the mission property and gather in these small cells, sometimes under a tree, sometimes directly beneath my window so that I could hear their discussions and see their enthusiasm.

The purpose of the meetings, I learned, was threefold: first, to study the newest Party directives or the speeches of Mao Tse-tung or Chu En-lai; secondly, to make plans for spreading these new instructions among the villages in our area; and thirdly, to learn songs and speeches to teach the people to whom they were sent.

Within the cell, it is the leader who is responsible for all activity. The cell leaders used to meet with *their* superiors once a week and make reports on the work of their cells.

A major part of these "leader meetings" was occupied with the personal reports and the confessions of the cell members. These were no high pressure self-accusations. They were *jen tso* or *tze jen* (confession of faults or self-confession). One officer told me, "It's just like your own Catholic Church confession."

So, there they did "Penance" after the washing of the brain ceremony (or "Baptism") had been performed. Public confession and self-imposed penances were announced to those present. And "Confirmation" of their ideas was going on incessantly.

One late afternoon, in a cell meeting under my window, I saw a young soldier arise and begin his list of "faults" committed since the last cell meeting, opportunities he had missed and mistakes he had made. He kicked the ground nervously as he went on. His big fault he said, was that two days ago, he had borrowed a wash basin from a family in town and he had not yet returned it. He must have forgotten about it, he explained, but in the morning he would certainly get it back.

The cell leader then asked, "What else are you going to do besides return the basin?"

The soldier said: "As a penance, I shall take only one bowl of rice this evening for my supper instead of the usual two."

The leader came back quickly and said: "Look, not only will you do that, but tomorrow you will not eat at all as a penance for your fault."

In this way was ruthless discipline maintained among the ardent members of the cells and within the army. And, of course, there was considerable honesty in these confessions, because often another member would remind the penitent of a fault should he have failed to confess it. It was obvious that these young people dreaded the moment when they were called upon to confess. I admired their willingness to go through with it, and I admired the genius of the Red leaders who knew how important it was to create deep conviction and strong discipline. It was a common expression of the people to say how courteous and honest were the new soldiers and the new Youth Corps.

I remember hearing a soldier pleading one evening with our cook not to report him or make known his serious crime to the officers: he had broken a water bottle in our kitchen.

To those who do not understand Communism it may sound fantastic when I tell you of a young girl who, with bowed head, confessed to her cell members: "I am ashamed, Comrades, but I must confess that at my father's execution I felt sadness in my heart and when I returned to my room I wept for him. Yet I know that this was wrong, for my father was a reactionary and an enemy of the People's Government, and so my enemy too."

Even one's secret thoughts and secret sins against the Cause were matter for confession.

Perhaps that is the reason why, in the beginning, for everything taken from our house by the Reds, we received a receipt—though, after the first month or so nothing was ever returned; the constant changing of personnel made it impossible for us to check on anything. The Reds would fly into a rage when I would tell them not to bother writing a receipt, for it meant nothing to me since I had already a large stack of them.

Later on, as the first teams moved on and lesser lights took over, ordinary soldiers would "borrow" things without any attempt to write a receipt. I was told that such practices were not allowed in the market place or in the villages—nothing was to be taken from the people, unless, of course, they happened to be landowners. The people were to see only the Communist "Sunday best"; the Reds managed by a Spartan discipline to conceal from many of the peasants the wolf fangs under their sheep's clothing.

CHAPTER SIX

Young Apostles

WHILE IT IS true that in our Tung-an area there were none of the wealthy landowners for which China is supposed to be so infamous, we did have some of those who were poorer than the others. There were also a number of farmers who had a small plot or two that they rented to poorer peasants. It seemed a poor spot for arousing the poor against the rich, for the simple reason that there were no rich and no really poor, or so we thought.

Still, there were farmers who owed rice; there were those who had bought on terms buffalo and pigs to replenish those lost during the Japanese occupation of Tung-an. Three years before the Communists took over, we had had a bad drought and the crops had been scanty, with the result that many of the poor had been refused loans by the shopkeepers and the better-off farmers, and for a time there was a bitterness in the hearts of many. These were the abuses on which the Reds later fed.

Such minor difficulties produced fertile enough soil for the

Reds to plant their seeds of resentment and jealousy and hatred. The cleavage was drawn, the smoldering embers fanned, the sides were lined up. There were, for the first time, two classes of people in Tung-an—the landlord class and the worker-peasant class, the haves and the have-nots, the creditors and the debtors.

With the setting up of the new People's Government it was announced that all these "unjust" debts need not be paid; that those who had not sufficient land would get what they needed. These people were to become the great "unarmed", who would be willing to do the bidding of the "armed" and their bosses, the top Party clique at the apex of the pyramid.

The Youth Corps members and the soldiers carried out their assignments well in sowing their seeds of strife. Soon village opposed village; old grievances were trotted out; family attacked family; children quarrelled openly with parents; brother was lined up against brother. In such an atmosphere as this, with distrust and hatred in the heart and on the tongue, it was a simple enough task to arrange "public accusation meetings" for those who wished to aid the People's Government and eliminate "injustices".

Often Red soldiers with the bait of a bit of candy would pump the children about their parents' conversations. Sometimes they would point to their guns and say: "I'm sure you don't have anything like this in your house." And if the child said: "Yes, my father has one," the soldiers would make a note of the man's name and bring him before the people for trial. Then they would make the child repeat the statement at a public gathering. In many cases I learned that the child's father actually did not have a gun; the child had made the claim merely (as children sometimes do) boastingly. But the boast would cost the father his life. For a child's statement is considered evidence enough to convict a victim in "democratic" China.

The older youngsters, the Youth Corps, had a more important duty. They together with the soldiers and propaganda teams were to suppress all reactionary thoughts, lest they be permitted to spread. These young people were encouraged to use any method to discover and suppress ruthlessly, but not *too* brutally, these thoughts, and also to remold the minds of the people. The Youth Corps was made to realize that patiently and perseveringly, through criticism and self-criticism, they were to bring about this change.

I was beginning to see—in my own case, and in the accusations carried on outside my window—that the methods used were well thought out and made use of violence. The "enemy", once suspected, must have his thoughts suppressed, his brain washed, and must be transformed into another man; or, if he had gone too far or was unwilling to change, he would be ruthlessly put away. I have seen some of these men come before the people at accusation meetings—later I was to see it all too closely in my own case—to be accused of "crimes" they could never have committed.

It was impossible for me, as I watched these well-trained youths perform their inhuman tasks, to minimize the seriousness of their convictions and the thoroughness of their methods. These convictions were deeply impressed on their minds; I prayed each day that the impression might not prove indelible.

Negatively speaking, no contrary thought is permitted, expressed or otherwise. Radical ideas must be suppressed; they are not to be expressed in public or published in the press or even voiced in private. Everyone has the duty of denouncing and waging war against such ideas. It soon became obvious that anyone who dares to profess ideas differing from those of the regime exposes himself to grave danger. Outside the accepted Communist teachings there is a complete intellectual blackout. The suppression of the source of information is the beginning of the conquest. After the brain is washed, there is a *tabula rasa* ready for the new impression; a need and an emptiness are created and Communism is to fill this void. How can these young people, looking at the world through rose—or Red—colored glasses, know that there is any other color? They know only one point of view—the Party's. They know only one morality, expediency, only one objective, success in the world revolution. No "troublesome" or reactionary thoughts such as I may have expressed to my people are permissible. That is why I was confined to my room—and alone.

The new ideas and strange thoughts are unconditionally accepted by the young, and accepted with a fanaticism which fears neither suffering, hardship nor death. I saw shy youths changed into courageous apostles; I saw the ambitious and selfish give up their goals and possessions; I saw some of my Christian youths break the bonds of family and friendship for this Cause.

The youth of Tung-an (later I found out it was the same with all the youth of China) had their ideals changed through criticism of self, as well as of others. In public and in the open, orally or with the pen, errors are thus corrected. By this personal reflection the ideas of the Party penetrate into the consciences of the members. It became clear to me that these master strategists understood thoroughly that once personal conviction has been established, future action would be directed by the principles and the ideology already inculcated. The lives of the youth would be overflowing with zeal for the Party. They are made to enter into the thoughts and feelings of the exploited and the poor. It is not enough that they understand their doctrine. They must also feel it convincingly and live it passionately. In China everyone is totally and totalitarianly organized for the purpose of complete conquest.

My own country, I began to see, was hated by these young zealots not only because they thought America had dealt unjustly with China and exploited her, but because these young men and women were convinced that our government and a few wicked capitalists were bleeding the world's poor of every ounce of blood and strength. They were the champions of the exploited workers—so they were taught and so they believed. I could feel their deep conviction of hatred against imperialists and exploiters, their love for the new People's Government and the revolution that had made it possible. They were confident with the confidence that comes with union and strength, and the sense of being a part of something big and new and good.

Their tired legs and muddy shoes, their calloused hands and eager eyes were testimonies of their conviction and I could understand the readiness of these youngsters to give evidence against their fellow villagers, their friends and their family. Only this could make the accusation meetings possible.

The accusers were seldom timid. They knew their parts well and spoke sharply the proper Party phrase at the proper time with the proper emphasis. The endless repetition of slogans and formulas, of lies and objectives, made these clichés a part of the daily life of the people. Like the theme of a symphony, pet grievances ran through all these accusations. In the preparatory meetings which were held hour-on-end on the mission property outside my west window, I heard these phrases daily like cacophonous calypso music repeated and repeated ad nauseam. The theme so often heard and seen and written and spoken was retained, as I could see when the same youth took the stand at the formal trials staged outside my east window to accuse the victims, who were sometimes members of his own family.

It is not by chance that these master indoctrinators use the public stage on which to accuse those who are guilty of thoughts or crimes against the People or the People's Government. This is dramatized action, drama to which the audience *must* come, a suspense play in which they must take an active part. They are the judge and the jury; they express their claims and their feelings; they pass down sentence and have their vengeance. This produces powerful reactions in them; they are reminded of their own misery and pains when a landlord is accused of unjust dealings. Weary and bent from toil they become conscious of their own trials when they see a worker accuse his employer of underpaying him.

After witnessing these accusation meetings and hearing many sentences of imprisonment and banishment to the mines or execution passed on the helpless victims, I began to experience a feeling of pity for the accused and a thought of fear for myself, wondering if one day I should have to endure a mob made mad by false accusations against *me*.

But as I watched the fury of the meetings slowly cool down and the crowds break up, I also asked myself what must be the thoughts of these simple folk who seemingly passed the sentence. Except for the Youth Corps members, there was obviously no feeling of triumph on their faces once the curtain fell on the drama. There was a look of fear—and sometimes guilt—as they silently walked away, back to their own homes and villages. Were they wondering if possibly they would be next? Each one seemed to be examining his own conscience to try to discover what might be there that could be adjudged contrary to the ideas of the Party. Perhaps they were trying to discover how convincingly they had accepted the new way of life; and perhaps they were trying to determine how much of the old life they still dared cling to. Maybe they asked themselves if any part of what they retained, any pre-Red thoughts or longings, could be discovered by those who watched them.

If they could not hate themselves for the old ideas that remained in their hearts, we can imagine them whispering to themselves: "The *real* I is not yet completely dead." This must have been possible, I knew, only for the older people. It would seem that the children now judged everything in a new light. The young could not hide even their innermost thoughts from those who directed their soulless lives. They could not hide them if they tried; their part was played too much in the public eye; their minds were read daily in the intimacy of friends and cell members. Secret sighs, murmurings in one's sleep, restlessness at discussion meetings—all these were watched by those whose duty it was to pry into each man's most secret self. Sooner or later you might give in, break down and confess. If you could not accept the new way you took your life or attempted an almost impossible escape.

Sometimes I would ask myself if these young people fully accepted everything that was taught them abut the hopes and ideals of Communism. It was difficult to doubt that they did. In the beginning many followed the "liberators" from fear; and I know they understood at once that an open denial of the Communist teachings or even a doubt displayed before their teachers was impossible. They realized that for them it was a question of acceptance or death. It was the only road open to them, so they traveled it and hoped for safety, peace and liberation. Once on this road it was impossible—or almost so—to turn back, or even to hesitate; one's whole self was carried along with the tide and one began very quickly to breathe the air of a new authority and new vigor and new union. I watched reluctance change to willingness and willingness to eagerness.

The Party's enemies became the enemies of each individual; the Party's point of view, his point of view; the Party's objective, his goal.

That helped me to understand the sacrifice these young people were making. I could see that their conversion was accomplished only by suffering, by long fatiguing hours of study and training. Not mere *listening* to the words of the instructor was required, but discussing his ideas and expressing one's opinion publicly and getting one's misunderstandings cleared up so that one *felt* the doctrine and became eager and restless to impart it to others.

These young cell members convening under my window often humiliated themselves before the others—confessing their past "criminal" offenses against the People. They told with shame of the doubts they might at first have had concerning the new regime. They testified to the reactionary sentiments of their parents, and soon began openly to hate them and all they stood for. For them these parents were simply in the way of the People's Revolution. These young people had to spy on their friends and their family—a task at first repulsive, but later entered into with zest. They prodded themselves to keep up with the feverish activity of the other young Reds, to keep up with the pace of the leaders, a pace which never slowed down for the laggards.

Of course, I know that these young people for years had been taught in their textbooks that they were slaves—slaves of the exploiters from the West, slaves of the landlords, slaves of the soil. Now, with the arrival of the "liberators," into their eyes there came a startled look of joy at being saved, at having escaped the web of the old dead customs which had kept them and their people prisoners. They seemed flushed with the success of the opening battle. They had seen some progress, some tangible signs of strength and service to their people. They manifested a strong faith in the ultimate triumph of their cause; and for that cause no sacrifice was too great, no effort too much, because it meant liberation for the millions of the poor all over the world—*their* masters would one day be the masters of all people everywhere.

As in every Communist state their agent of progress was organized and systematized violence. From this flowed logically the ruthless savagery of absolute dictatorship, unjust and unjustifiable executions, and bitter enslavements. This atheist-materialist philosophy of violence taught these young zealots that the process must inevitably continue until a world-wide dictatorship of the same kind is achieved. Until this goal is reached there can be no rest, no peace. Everything non-Communist must be violently destroyed.

When I reflected on these simple facts of history these tireless youths made more sense to me. I could understand better the bitterness of their accusations, and the thoroughness with which they ferreted out those who would not accept the "saving doctrine." These were the reasons one must wage such a deathless struggle: a struggle with oneself first of all, and then with all the enemies of the cause from within and from without.

I tried to uncover, as I watched these youths, the psychological techniques that were being employed to refashion them. Their propaganda leaders and indoctrinators were, I conceded, past-masters in the art of organizing the masses. They gave to each group the respective hope each class longed to attain—for the intellectual, equality; for the landless, land; for the youth, a cause; for the children, ideals.

I found myself asking: how long? How long will their zeal

remain? Will it last when the fervor of the police action cools and slackens? Only then will I know how really deep is the conviction and how sincere the conversion. But for the moment from my prison window I had to watch and admire and fear the ceaseless, burning activity of those who had been set on fire.

No one anywhere could have had a better view of these youth meetings than I had; and nowhere could their zeal be more manifest than at the open-air trials by the side of the road which I could watch from my east window. Here the dreaded accusation meetings were carried on day after day until I wondered if in the whole valley there could be another person left to endure the agony of exposure to this mob roused to white anger by mere youth as it accused the enemies of the People.

Here, too, one could obtain vengeance for wrongs long harbored in one's heart. I saw wives testify against husbands who, they said, had aided guerrillas. I saw poor peasants accuse farmers who, they claimed, had exacted exorbitant interest. I saw tenant farmers who charged their landlords with asking excessive rent. While some of these charges were in part true, most of them were due to petty jealousies. Some who had no grievances but who were anxious to aid the Cause were prompted by propagandists to accuse a suspect the Reds wished done away with.

Having mastered the "Agitators' Handbook," the Youth Corps would find no great problem in pitting a village against its neighboring village. I was told of a grievance in two nearby villages that had been almost forgotten for thirty years. The Reds found out about it and this ancient dispute over the flow of drainwater was made the issue in the trial and accusation of the leading family in each of the two villages. The Reds, of course, were on the side of the poorer peasants and championed their cause even though in this case the cause was quite unjust. . . .

Parents began to tremble with fear every time they saw their children talking with Red soldiers or with members of the Youth Corps. They would, in the beginning, call them away and put them to work, afraid even to tell the child the reasons for their fear. In many accusation meetings they had heard other children and young people willingly and brazenly accusing their parents of reactionary crimes. They had seen children loudly applauded and generously awarded for every revelation of village faults or murmurings against the People's Government. Love of country was the first and only love. There are few secrets in a Chinese village. Nothing is hidden—the village is but one big family. The Chinese often repeat the proverb: "When the baby is spanked, the whole village weeps." What a perfect field for trouble seekers!

In the early days of the "liberation" of Tung-an I saw a good Catholic friend of mine executed. I found out later that a twelve-year-old girl had publicly but unjustly accused him of dealing with anti-Communist forces. She stated that she had overheard him telling other men about his plans to aid the guerrilla forces. That was enough to convict him, incredible though it may seem.

The precocious child, as the Reds know so well, delights in the attention showered upon him by adults, and the flattery heaped upon such child "heroes" after an accusation meeting was obsequious to an extreme. Children in the new regime were, temporarily at least, given a great deal of authority. Their tiny fingers might at any moment be directed at an adult, and, if the authorities had any reason to put the accused away the child was brought on the stage to testify against him. Even on the streets the youngsters had the right (which they delighted to use) to search adults for anti-Communist papers or guns.

From my window overlooking the bus road and the accusation stage I could see the teams of youngsters gang up on an adult, curse him and ridicule him. They would request adults to show their passes, and the soldiers standing nearby would smile approvingly as the children performed their unfilial duties.

Gone was the old reverential respect the children had for their elders, gone was the ancient and natural authority of parents over their children. In fact the old delightful niceties of Chinese etiquette had been "washed away" too. No longer did one hear: "What is your honorable name? Where is your honorable ancestral home?" It became merely: "What's your name? Where are you from?" No longer was the tea cup presented and received standing with both hands extended. Cigarettes were handed with two fingers or tossed to the recipient. Always the Youth Corps and the soldiers would ridicule the refined social customs of the old polite China, and no one dared to be heard or seen using them. Once parental authority had been crushed, there were no lessons learned except those given the child by the master propagandists through their agents in the school or in the army. Their new instructors had sold China's glorious cultural birthright for a "mess of verbiage."

CHAPTER SEVEN

The Drums of Ten Tan Ko

TUNG-AN NEVER needed a prison until Tung-an went Red. And it is an ironical fact that the first prison in Tung-an was the "Lord of Heaven's Hall"—the Catholic Church. Our hearts bled when we saw the black and red altars and church benches carried away. Stocks were substituted for the benches, chains for the kneelers, and Mao replaced Christ in the sanctuary. Spittle and mud marred the clean surface of the sanctuary floor.

For over a year political prisoners had either been sent off to the county seat or been held in a small house in our market-town. But now the system was clicking; cells were ferreting out reactionaries; guerrillas were being rounded up. So our church was considered the most suitable place for the increased number of criminals.

Normally the church seated about 250 Christians for ceremonies. We were told, after the first week of operations, that over two hundred prisoners were incarcerated there. Each group of four prisoners would be fitted at their ankles into a stock (until they ran out of stocks) and assigned space along the wall sufficient only for each man to lie down, locked and unable to move. Those without stocks were chained and given space in the middle of the church or in the sanctuary. I began to understand what the two-party Communist Democracy meant: one party in power, the other in prison!

From our west window I could see these helpless innocent men pushed through the mission gates. I recognized so many—they were not just people, they were friends of mine, Christians of mine, men with whom I had sipped tea, men whom I had healed in our dispensary. What was their crime? Merely that they were known not to like atheistic Communism, or that they were *suspected* of not liking it—which in the mind of the Reds was the same thing. Or maybe they were thought to have information of value to the regime.

As I paced the pine board floor of my comfortable prison room in the rectory, my heart went out to these political prisoners in my church. The groans floated up from the doors and windows, and the wailing and groaning and occasional shrieking went on all day and all night. Some nights it would be impossible for me to sleep, and my nerves became jumpy from the misery that was there.

One day as I passed by the church on my way to the open public toilet, the cries of two prisoners attracted my attention. I saw two men strung up by their thumbs to a hook on the wall, their toes barely touching the floor—a most cruel torture designed to extort a confession. The other prisoners cursed them for their loud wailing, for their nerves were worn thin also.

Never in the United States have I heard a man wail or groan like this. Perhaps this sound is peculiar to the oriental—a low moaning mixed with unintelligible curses. The misery of this prison attested to a state of human degradation I had never dreamed possible.

Occasionally I would ask the guards assigned to watch me what the cause of some unusual wailing would be, and they would laughingly say: "Oh, some enemy of the People's Government refuses to confess so they've tied him up by the thumbs—that makes a man say what we want to know." To have shown the slightest pity would have been unworthy of a soldier of the new Red China. I know of one Christian who went eight days thus strung up before he eventually died.

The main door of the prison church had been sealed up with bricks. Only the small side door leading to the sacristy was used by the prisoners. The public open toilet was a long trench dug along the mission wall near the rectory. Early in the morning the prisoners, six or eight at a time, were allowed out for a few brief moments to take care of nature's needs and to get a breath of fresh air and a few steps to exercise their weakening muscles.

I could see each debased prisoner clearly as he came out, and could see that a number of them were our Christians. I saw the Catholic in whose home the Sisters had taken momentary refuge when they were expelled from their convent. That apparently was crime enough to impound him in the cesspool that once was the House of God. His hair, like that of the others, was long and shaggy down the back of his neck; a few strands of gray beard fell from his chin. One morning I saw him assisting another prisoner whose feet and legs were pitifully bloated with beri-beri. The guard prodded them to move faster, since their time out in the open was limited. All of these men looked haggard and hopeless; obviously some were dying from the poor food and lack of air.

It was quite a simple matter for the Communists to run the

jail. It cost very little. The buildings were confiscated property, the guards were few, and the food was supplied by the families of the condemned. Each day I would see the sad line of wives and children and mothers coming to bring rice to their husbands, fathers, or sons. Each visitor was searched and each food pail inspected by the guards. The food was brought only as far as the mission gate, then the name of the prisoner was told to the guard, who would bark out the name and hand the food to a trusty who took it to the prisoner in the church. The families lingered at the gate hoping to get a glimpse of their loved ones imprisoned inside. For a while the women and children came twice a day, but later this was reduced to once a day—and later I saw fewer and fewer children, because, no doubt, they found it too embarrassing listening to the taunts of their friends about their prisoner fathers or elder brothers.

One day I noticed a number of local youths helping the soldiers do guard duty—this was a temporary privilege preparatory to entering the army. Among the new guards I noticed A-Tao, a young man who used to come frequently to the mission dispensary. I knew his father and mother well. It surprised me one morning to see A-Tao's father come out of the church with the other prisoners. About an hour later I was going to the lavatory; on the way I passed A-Tao doing guard duty.

"A-Tao," I whispered, "what has your father done that he should be imprisoned with the men in the church?"

"That is not my father," was the astonishing reply A-Tao gave me.

Then I took pains to watch A-Tao as his father came out each day. The guards were expected to yell and curse at the prisoners and mercilessly hurry them along. A-Tao would treat his father the same as the others—perhaps a little worse than the others, to show how worthy he was to become accepted into the

People's army. It turned my stomach to watch this transformation of all that in old China had stood for the noble relationship between father and son.

Not all the prisoners in the church were men. The sacristy had been converted into a prison for women. About ten women were confined there. One or two were there because of some personal crime against the Party, but most of them because their suspected husbands had fled. These wives were held as hostages until their return. One of these women, I recall, was very old and feeble; but most of them were young women who were forced to do such work as carrying water and cleaning the property. One woman had her little two- or three-year-old boy with her, and his was the only baby voice in all that din of deep moaning and wailing.

There is no way to describe the anguish that filled my heart as I watched and listened to these men and women in the church prison. At night when their cries cut the black silence, I would try to distinguish the voices and wonder if it might be that one of my Christians was suffering because he had shielded or defended me. How the families of these men must have suffered—wives and mothers who daily braved the insults and taunts of the soldiers to bring rice to their loved ones.

I recall the day I looked out the east window toward the market place and saw soldiers busily constructing the public trial stage by the road no more than forty yards from my room. At first I thought I was going to have a boxseat at some of the Communist propaganda plays which I had heard were so powerful in swaying the people. The twenty-foot platform was arranged so that the audience stood in the dry field off the road. At the back of the crude platform, suspended on bamboo poles, were pictures of Mao Tse-tung and Stalin; there were no other drapes or decorations.

The day the stage was completed gave me an indication of what sort of drama was to be enacted before my eyes. Two prisoners were led from the church—an elderly man and a fine-looking youth of about eighteen. I recognized the older man as a person whom everyone pointed to as a ne'er do well, but the boy was a good lad.

It was a market day. The soldiers hustled the pair through the gathered populace and ushered them onto the stage. A considerable crowd collected and an officer spoke to them about the prisoners' crimes. Then a man in civilian clothing got up and spoke. He accused the two prisoners of anti-Communist activities and refusal to confess or amend their lives. Without any further questioning or ceremony the soldiers took over and right before my eyes the two men, hands tied behind their backs, were forced to kneel down in the field about ten feet from the stage. Five soldiers leveled their guns and, at a bark from the officer in charge, fired a volley of bullets into the two prisoners. Their bodies lay there in the field untouched for three days.

The next market day, three days later, as the people from the villages filed along the road to the town, I noticed the soldiers near the mission direct them into the field in front of the stage. They were to witness the process of justice in their new Communist state. They were to take part in the trial of two of their own. Mass terror was the prescribed means to subdue all opposition.

Two bound prisoners taken from the church were brought to the stage. They were placed before a table in back of which sat a Red official and two aids. One assistant stood and read from a paper the crimes of the victims. Two people in the audience stood up and seemed to second the statement read by the official. No other witnesses came forth to accuse the condemned. The judge, after hearing the statement, asked the people what punishment should be given. The spontaneous reply came promptly: "*Sa! Sa!*" ("Kill! Kill!") The two men were then led through the crowd and about twenty feet beyond, directly under my window and in full view of the people, soldiers placed their guns against the backs of their heads and fired. Then the soldiers and children gathered over the bodies, the masterpieces of God's creation, and the youngsters kicked at them.

In the beginning it seemed that only school children and members of the Youth Corps cried out the sentences; they quickly became calloused to the sight of death. It took longer to get the adults into the spirit of the drama, but after a bit of prodding by the soldiers and a few pointed questions from the officials, all automatically got in on the act. I could see the hopeless expressions on the faces of these men who were on trial for their lives, on trial without benefit of counsel. Since all lawyers were government servants, what attorney would dare oppose the government in favor of a client? Nor could the accused utter a word in his own defense. Hands tied behind his back, usually kneeling before the people, the criminal was abused, kicked and condemned before a word could be spoken.

I could feel the anger of the people being kindled, and I could see pair after pair of prisoners brought to the spot by my window to be killed. These were not for me names in the morning paper—these were men I knew, men I had taken care of in my dispensary. As time passed many were Christians who had called me their Spiritual Father.

Each market day after the people had made their purchases, they knew that they were expected to gather in the field near the mission. The Youth Corps members would round them up. These enthusiastic young men came down the road to the rhythm of drums—banners and streamers flying, the marchers doing the Yangko dance as they came, strutting and dipping as the procession moved to the stage. The monotonous beat of these drums went on then throughout the day and part of the night—*da-da-dum, da-da-dum, da-da-dum, dum, dum.*

These same trials and executions were going on in other villages throughout the valley—and, I later learned, in *every* market town throughout China. The crowds increased from market day to market day—those who stayed away were under suspicion. A ruthless campaign of suppression, a bloodthirsty spectacle like those of pagan Rome, was being carried on before my eyes. The women and children were requested to wear gay colored clothes. Each village was given a distinctive color, and the dancers would wear sashes and wave banners bearing the color of their village.

The accusations became better timed and the speeches of the judges more passionate as the trials continued. No opportunity was missed to impress upon the people the seriousness of the crimes and the need for the full punishment. After each pronouncement of "death to the landlord," or "death to the reactionary," the people would let out a tremendous cheer, not unlike a college cheering section at a football game in America. It was a frenzied crowd, led by a Youth Corps member with raised clenched fist, shouting Communist slogans: "Mao Tse-tung, ten thousand years!" The shout was the cheer of victory —the shrill, exciting cry of triumph.

After about six weeks the executions were turned over to the local Agricultural Society. Then it became neighbor executing neighbor—relative executing relative. In the beginning I would make a mark on the wall to keep count of the number killed under my window. The number on the wall reached 76 before the rains came and the low fields flooded and the stage was moved to the higher ground on the other end of the town. But by that time I had already seen far too much. And by that time the political criminals had been pretty well cleared out. After about a month or so at the other end of the town the executions dwindled to an occasional objector.

It was a soldier who told me that what I saw going on outside my window in Tung-an was being repeated in hundreds of places throughout the Southwest. And later when I spoke in Hong Kong to other priests it became apparent how vast must have been the total number of executions. One market place near Tung-an had seen twenty-one killed in one day—or so a soldier triumphantly reported to me. It was easy to calculate several hundred executions in our small area of Tung-an. What must it have been for the whole province of Kwangsi, to say nothing of the entire country! The Sisters' convent was the headquarters for this whole area and soldiers and officials came here to make their reports. Always they would come to my quarters to see the "Southwest China spy leader," as I was now called. On these visits they would boast of the number of criminals executed in the various villages under their command. No doubt it was done to allow me time to think over my own fate, should I remain unwilling to confess *my* crimes.

What puzzled me at first was the enthusiasm of the people when they rose, hands extended, and shouted for the death of the criminal. I could see that the propagandists and the judge were master rabble rousers, and they knew well the psychology of the mob. Some witnesses, no doubt, realized that if they did not join in the unjust shouts for the death of an innocent man, they themselves would be under suspicion. No one knew the thoughts of the person standing next to him, and each one was thinking of his own life and doing everything possible to preserve it.

As I watched these "trials" in which the State acted as witness, prosecutor and judge, my mind went back to our American way. I thought of every American's privilege of standing on his "constitutional rights."

The Police of the Red regime have thoroughly mastered the technique of detecting crime and those suspected of crime. Red practice, however, will not permit an officer to take any step that might seem to protect the innocent. It is not only the deed itself which is the object of Red China's penal laws, it is the will of the criminal that is considered. If he is regarded a potential danger to the State he must be eliminated. The unfortunate moment for these "criminals" is not the moment they become guilty of an act, but the moment they are considered dangerous to society.

There was never a market day passed but that I thought my turn was next. My prayer was—little dreaming what lay ahead of me—that I would be spared the humiliation of a trial before the people. A quick, clean-cut death would be easy, but never the trial before the people.

At dusk I would watch from my window as sad silent figures moved stealthily toward the corpses of the executed, still lying where they dropped in the field. They were the wives or mothers of the dead, carrying some rice straw and a homemade stretcher to bring back the corpses of their loved ones. Sometimes a woman would throw herself hysterically down by the side of a corpse and sob herself weak. Some would look from side to side, fearful of detection, but with love strong enough to brave the danger to give their dear ones the final respect of burial. The bodies would be bundled up in the rice straw, rolled on the stretcher, and carried away into the darkness.

It was with mingled feelings of disgust and pity that I watched the children climb on the stage to play after the accusation meetings and the executions. They called their game "wo-pa" (the bad man) and engaged in it much as American youngsters might play at "cops and robbers." These children would go through a whole mock trial in perfect imitation of the real thing they had watched earlier in the day. They would force the "condemned" child to kneel, and would strike him on the back of the neck, then kick him and drag him off the stage, where a mock execution would take place accompanied with fiendish cheers. These calloused and cold-blooded performances often were witnessed by a few amused and approving soldiers.

There was an occasional beheading among the executed. These ordinarily were major offenders—guerrilla leaders, anti-Communist promoters, and one or two of the wealthier farmers. This procedure sent a cold shock up my spine each time I saw the long machete-like knife called for and the victim kneel and bow his head. Then came the most gruesome gesture of the whole inhuman performance: the heads were taken and suspended by ropes on a wooden frame at the entrance to the market place that looked like football goal-posts. At the side of the upright posts were written the crimes of the victims.

These heads would hang there for several weeks. People coming to and going from market would glance up at the gruesome sight, shudder and shy as far away from them as possible, or spit on the ground and rush by. Sometimes women from distant villages would even turn around and go home rather than pass by them.

But here again the youth were different. They stood in front of the "goal-posts" and made remarks about the victim, and obviously gloated over the fact that the criminal had been put to death. One day a soldier called me to the window and pointed to the row of heads: "Look, have you seen the new heads that have been strung up today? That will teach any objectors the power of the new People's Government." His satanic laugh sent a chill through me.

Lesser criminals, or those who were not completely converted, were given minor sentences. The guards told me of coal and iron mines that were being opened in Southwest China, to which many less important criminals were sent. The guards explained to me that the government "benevolently fed and clothed these men!" I knew the type of men sent off to the mines; most of them were minor officials in the Nationalist Government or small shopowners who had never done manual work before. It was obvious that many of them would soon die there.

Some of the lesser criminals kept at Tung-an had to do menial work about the mission or in the town. Their crimes were written on large placards hanging from their shoulders, like the sign of the sandwich man back home. Women and children were encouraged to ridicule and torment them.

I can never recall these scenes on the stage without seeing in my mind a young woman from the house of Chang.

She was very friendly with the Sisters and stayed with them for some time after the Reds came into Tung-an. She used to bring her sickly three-year-old son often to the dispensary, and repeatedly said that we had saved his life. And she was most grateful. One day before our dispensary was closed, she came for medicine. The soldiers on guard stopped her and questioned her: "Why do you come to this foreigner for medicine?"

"I am a very poor woman," she explained in a loud defiant voice, "and I have no money to go elsewhere. Besides, where in the whole area am I able to go for medicine for my son?"

"You should see the local officials—they will direct you to a local doctor," was the soldiers' reply.

"What difference does it make," she asked, "so long as the priest is willing and able to help me?"

After entering the dispensary she continued to talk about the unreasonableness of the guards, and I motioned to her to be quiet for fear the soldiers would come and expel her. But she was defiant and fearless.

A week later I heard that the Reds had taken her to the prison in the county seat of Ping-lo. Then several months later I was shocked to hear that she had become the leader of the village Communist Women's Society.

Not long afterwards on a market day there seemed to be more excitement than usual in the large crowd in the field by my window. Three "criminals" were tried for acts of treason. All three naturally were condemned to be executed. In the ordinary manner the soldiers put their guns to the heads of two of the victims, then there was a delay and an excited murmur went through the crowd.

The young woman, who a few months before had stood in our dispensary berating and cursing the Communists and all they stood for, came forth and received a gun from one of the soldiers. She held it defiantly to the back of the prisoner's head and pulled the trigger. She showed no signs of nervousness or remorse as she walked away amid the cheers of the mob. She took her little boy by the hand and departed.

It was obvious that if she was to become a real leader of the women she must show her fearlessness. She must be a living exemplar for the new China's womanhood. This was what the Reds meant by the "equality of the sexes." Saturated with atheism and coarse ideas the women of Tung-an, if they followed this woman of the house of Chang, would lose, I felt sure, all that was tender and all that was beautiful in womanhood and motherhood. Several times after that demonstration of brutality by the Chang woman soldiers told me of this woman's wonderful courage. It proved, they said, that women were as brave as men and as fearless. Officials would praise her in their speeches and point to her as an example for all women.

Before each accusation meeting and at the conclusion of the executions the Youth Corps would perform their Yangko dance. At first the older people frowned upon it because it was foreign to China and to the old Chinese mind—actually there were no folk dances in old China. Young men would dress as women, children would follow the Youth Corps and mimic the steps and echo the drums. Later girls participated.

The Youth Corps and soldiers would spend hours teaching the steps to new recruits or to the children. They would practice at night and go out into the villages to teach it to others. Coming along the road to the accompaniment of the drums, each village would wear its own color. In caricature, at the head of the line, would be Chiang Kai-shek or his wife or Uncle Sam.

The youngsters loved it. Night after night I would hear the drums from as far away as the village of Ten Tan Ko. It wore on my nerves. I often hoped that the incessant beating of the drums would stop just for one night. The rhythm was western, the dance was western, there was nothing oriental about it. But the noise and the color and the excitement caught on, and many a peasant who was on the fence found it impossible not to be swayed into the Red camp by the contagious rhythm of the drums and the gay, triumphant accent of the dance.

CHAPTER EIGHT

The Mastermind

DURING APRIL 1951, after the heroic Chinese nuns and Fathers Nugent and Gilmartin had been expelled from the mission of Tung-an, the Red officials repeatedly told me that my permission to leave would be coming along from headquarters in a day or two.

Mr. Su, a suave, debonair, middle-aged man, whom I had met years before in Kweilin, came in frequently to see me in those days. He had been a rather well-to-do businessman in the pre-Communist era; but being shrewd, he sold out early and jumped on the Red bandwagon just in time to save his capitalist neck. He was a kindly sort of fellow who seemed to have considerable sympathy for me, especially when I narrated some of the difficulties I had had with the Red officials.

One day he asked me if I had any grievances against the men who were holding me prisoner. Perhaps I should have suspected him but I fell into the trap and spoke: "Only one that is serious. Ask them to permit me to carry on my work, and give tangible evidence of the meaning of the 'Freedom of Religion' sign on the mission wall."

Mr. Su replied: "That will be all cleared up shortly, as soon as the guerrillas are subdued in this area. Is there anything else that is wrong?"

Then naively I listed for him the insults inflicted on me by the soldiers and the Major in charge of the mission garrison. I told him of the many personal belongings that had been taken from me. I told him that the Major had occupied the mission property illegally and had destroyed our church. He made notes of my complaints and gave me the impression that the insults and offenses would end. I gave him the information, feeling that he was going to help me by reporting the situation to higher officials in Kweilin, who, I (wrongly, of course) thought, had no idea of the conditions in Tung-an. Only after several weeks did I learn to whom Mr. Su confided my confidential report. The Major was to have his revenge on me.

While Mr. Su was in Tung-an he used our rectory for his quarters. He and his guard and a big German police dog moved right in with me. Mr. Su was at that time directing a team of about eighty young men and women in the division of the fields in this district. At the same time he gave propaganda instructions and lectures to them. And, using me as a guinea pig, he showed the young people the proper procedure in getting information from a person. He also showed them the technique in searching a house—listing the contents. He asked me questions about everything under the sun—my personal life and my innermost thoughts.

I recall how amused I was one afternoon when Mr. Su brought a tall, overbearing Red official with a long drooping Fu-Manchu mustache into my quarters to see me. I was prepared for a ponderous inquisition from the impressive, stern-looking official. Mr. Su began showing him about, and suddenly they found a child's basketball game that I sometimes took on mission trips to amuse the children. It caught the imagination of the distinguished visitors and they sat down on the bed fascinated by the toy. The tiny mechanical basketball player tossing the ball toward the hoop when they flipped the lever so engrossed these two Communist officers that they forgot all about me and the purpose of their visit. No two American youngsters could have been more intently absorbed. The recollection of that scene in my prison room still makes me smile.

One day, while my guests were searching my room, I glanced up from a feeble attempt at reading to see Mr. Su take a photograph out of my trunk near the bed. "You were younger then, were you not?"

"Yes, Mr. Su, that is a picture taken at the time of my ordination—when I graduated from the seminary," I explained.

He said he would like to take it and an album of snapshots to headquarters to clear them with the authorities there. I could offer no reasonable objection, so he put them under his arm. Then he began to finger through a small box of medals that was on my dressing case. I watched him closely and I saw him hold in his hand two U.S. Army insignia and an army chaplain's cross. I had said Mass during the Japanese war for our American troops in Southwest China and, while not an official chaplain, I did have the chaplain's insignia. These seemed to fascinate Mr. Su and he looked long and musingly at them. Then I saw him take out of the box a large toy medal given to me by a small boy years ago as a souvenir when I left home for China. In the middle of the medal were the letters "U.S." and across the top in a semicircle were four blue stars. I had completely forgotten about it through the years; but it, too, seemed to intrigue Mr. Su, and I saw him, without any comment other than an amused smile, drop the big medal and the U.S. Army insignia into his pocket. The chaplain's cross he replaced in the box; and the box he replaced on the dresser.

Little did I realize that day the importance this scene was to play in my life before the Communists were through with me.

Mr. Su was acquainted with many of the other Maryknoll priests in this section of China, and through him I learned that all my neighbor priests had already been deported to Hong Kong.

"What of my bishop, Msgr. Romaniello, and the priests in Kweilin?" I asked him.

"They are very likely still in their mission," he answered.

"Then why not let me go there and permit me to be with the other priests?"

But Mr. Su would reply only vaguely to my question. Actually, as I found out later, he was lying to me, for all our priests had long since been deported.

Later that same day he came back with his personal bodyguard, a dull, halfwit type of lad who seemed awed in Mr. Su's presence, and never left his side. The squat, gnomelike guard looked around with obvious suspicion of me and everything in my room. After hearing him struggle to express his thoughts I had uncharitably dubbed him the "Mastermind." It was clear that the Mastermind's brain had not only been well washed, but a good part of it had been washed away.

Mr. Su said that all our belongings were to be stored in one room and locked. Mr. Su explained to me that since all Chinese assets in America had been frozen it was necessary for him to "freeze" my things. So the guard and I packed all my books and whatever other personal effects were left into the storeroom. A team of youngsters came in and listed everything. I managed to hold out the vestments and some wine and wheat for Mass, also the Bible and two spiritual books which I was able to hide in back of the bookshelves. The lock was big and strong, and I felt as though I had said goodbye to some close friends when Mr. Su finally snapped it close. He handed the keys to the Mastermind with a word of warning. That night as Mr. Su left my quarters he told me that any day now my permission to move to Kweilin would be coming on the bus from Ping-lo. Believing him, I gave away most of the money I had to a poor Catholic woman whose husband was in prison.

The Mastermind and his big German police dog then became my roommates and my guards; they ate with me, and slept on the floor in my room. The big dog caused me no concern though the fleas he carried would never stay on his fur. The Mastermind quickly sensed his supreme authority and loved to manifest his "superiority" over the other soldiers and students who came into my room. Whenever they wished to "borrow" anything now, I would refer them to the Mastermind, and he would always refuse. Not that there was much left now, but they would wish to get into the storeroom, and that he would never allow.

After a few days together I found that my guard was childishly simple at heart and I began even to like to hear him talk. He would tell me about his boyhood: "I never knew who my parents were," he would say, "they were killed by the Japanese years ago. As a small boy I was taken by the police to a town in Manchuria. I never went to school. I worked as an office boy sweeping up the floor and serving tea in a Communist headquarters. I just naturally grew up in the great Communist Party. Later I became a soldier in the Red army." And on and on he would go telling me many things in his unimaginative way. He would tell me about the Russians in Manchuria. "Could they eat," he said, "no Chinese can eat as much as a Russian!"

Having traveled all the way from Manchuria in the northeast down to Tung-an in the southwest as a private guard in the Red police, the Mastermind had seen considerable. As we sat in the room in the evening, he would stealthily open the storeroom and pour a glass of Mass wine—of which we still had a good quantity at the time. I encouraged him to sip the wine, because I knew it took only a bit to loosen his slow tongue. It was then that he would talk about the Russian soldiers and technicians and the Chinese Red officers he knew. He told me about the Church in North China, and it was from the Mastermind that I learned about the pressure on the Church, the persecutions of the Christians, and of the murder of several Chinese priests.

The dull-witted soldier didn't realize it, but he was giving me details of the mortal combat between the Hammer and Sickle and the Cross. He said these priests and Christians were put to death because they "refused to cooperate." I knew that they had been forced to pay the supreme price because they had put their God above the master of the Brute State.

My guard kept me informed of developments in Tung-an also. He would point out to me the various officers and their ranks. There is no clear way, from their dress or insignia, to distinguish officers in the Chinese Red army, but the Mastermind knew the "brass" and he seemed to take pleasure in pointing them out to me. Even though all in the Red army are equal, he explained that "actually there is a distinction in rank." He also knew the propaganda teams and their leaders. He went into detail about the different colored uniforms—the army and police in khaki, the propaganda teams in blue. He told me of the meager salary given to each soldier, but added that the government generously gave the members their clothes and some soap and toothbrushes, and that the village people "showed their love of the army by bringing in rice and vegetables for the soldiers."

Not long after the Mastermind moved in he developed a bad case of malaria, and he gave me the key to the storeroom so that I could get atabrine tablets for him. I would bathe him with cold towels once or twice a day to keep the fever down, and I would prepare rice for both of us. It made me feel good to help him; and it pleased me to see his sincere expression of gratitude.

I gave him some vitamins which he really seemed to need, and I took a few for myself from the storeroom at the same time. He later developed running sores around his mouth, and these sores plus his serrated teeth, and his dull-witted mind, made me very uneasy sometimes as I ate with him, sticking my chopsticks into our common bowl of green vegetables, and drinking from the same cup he used.

After he recovered, he used to sit by the hour telling me of the glories of Communism and Mao Tse-tung. While he made no direct attempt to convert me, I listened to keep him amiable and hoping he would continue to get things for me from the storeroom. He would often bring in propaganda team members to lecture me on Communist doctrine. But I tried not to listen to these "professionals."

The Mastermind seemed to take childish delight in showing groups of students or other soldiers through the room. He would point out the few possessions of mine that still remained and give the visitors the story on them as I had given it to him. By this time my room had become the Grand Central Terminal or the Grant's Tomb of Tung-an—a place everyone had to pass through, a sight every visitor had to see.

Sometimes Major Warsaw would come in with a group of young people, and he would demonstrate for their benefit the proper procedure in "washing the brain" of a foreigner. His clincher seemed to be: "Now look, you are an educated man, why don't you give up all this superstition and your work for the American imperialists?"

The Communist daily papers carried details about the "tremendous losses" America was suffering in its "hopeless struggle" in Korea; and of the large number of American prisoners "converted" to the Communist way of life. The daily bombings of innocent Chinese in Manchuria, and civilians in Korea were reported in these papers, and there were daily stories of rape and other atrocities committed against Koreans in the wartorn peninsula, and accounts of the "aims" of the American imperialists in China's Manchuria—and eventually in all of Asia.

The Press, as well as the Mastermind and the Youth Corps, spoke with conviction of the rising of China's sun and the decline of American greatness. The savior of China would lead China to the heights.

After the Mastermind's malaria cleared up he used to go out each day for a walk to the market place. That left me a few cherished moments to myself. The strain of the guard's constant stare and his unending questioning began to be like the pulling of a file over my tightly-drawn nerves, and I prayed to be left alone for at least a few minutes each day. Then I would sink to my knees and ask Our Lady to help me, to give me courage to stand the daily battle of nerves. With the guard and the dog in the room it was impossible for me to pray. He talked constantly. When he left me alone I could think of my Christians and the Chinese Sisters, and I would pray for them that they might be strong in the face of the overwhelming odds arrayed against them.

I seemed better able to stand the ordeals of the evenings after an hour or two alone. I felt stronger and better able to answer the propaganda leaders, and listen to the extolling of Mao, and even able to put my chopsticks in the vegetable bowl with the Mastermind, without so much uneasiness.

Gradually, from bits of news that my personal guard passed along to me over his evening cup of wine, I realized that all the Maryknoll Fathers had been expelled from Southwest China, and that I was the only priest in this entire area. I was glad in a sense that the others were freed and were able to carry on their priestly work elsewhere. Up until then had I felt that, even though no word came to me from my confreres, they were not far away and that one day soon when the bus came along with my permit to move on to Kweilin, I would see them. I don't think the Mastermind meant to taunt or frighten me, but it made me uneasy to hear him report: "Now you're the only foreigner left in these parts". It did make me feel terribly lonesome, and the loneliness seemed like a cloak that covered me completely. There was no one now in the whole area who would dare raise a voice in my behalf—almost every face I saw, every voice I heard, was that of an enemy.

Every once in a while—usually at night—my guard would bring me over to see the officials occupying the Sisters' Convent. They would carry on a routine schedule, asking me about my life, and my associations in America and in China. And they would put me through the usual session of indoctrination —usually done by an officer for the benefit of the young soldiers standing around. At least I always felt these doctrinal dissertations were meant for the others rather than for me.

One night they were telling me all about the recent atrocities committed by Americans against innocent Korean women and children. One of the soldiers, a rather tall stupid-looking country lad, listening for a bit, stuttered out in a stage whisper to the man next to him: "Korea, does that place belong to America?" There was an embarrassing silence and a few titters, and then one of the officials sharply replied: "Stupid, no, it does not belong to America, though America is trying to steal it from the Korean people. You should know this if you would follow the news reports attentively."

The youngster was quite simple in his attitude; he didn't seem to enjoy the joke. It was the only time I ever saw any signs of levity at a Communist meeting. The subject was passed off quickly and we went on to the matter at hand, after which they returned me to my room.

Apart from the young women of the Youth Corps, few women ever came to my quarters to inspect the place or to taunt me. Most of them were still too innately decent to invade my privacy. But one afternoon three soldiers came in followed by about fifteen village women. They seemed to be somewhat embarrassed but also quite curious to see me and to see my quarters. The soldiers took the occasion to explain to the women about the luxurious life led by the foreigner. They referred to a few objects still remaining in my room. The pagan women asked a number of questions about me and about my work, and these questions gave the soldiers a welcome opportunity to ridicule me and the Church and Imperialist America.

My deportation orders failed to come; the questionings failed to ease up; my nerves were wearing thin. At such times small inconveniences assumed disproportionate importance. As an instance I found the well by the gate house had had a cover put on it, with a lock. That night after his cup of wine the Mastermind confided in me that the Major had ordered the well locked because he was afraid that I might put poison in it and kill all the soldiers. So now whenever I wanted water for my cooking or washing I had to seek out the officer who kept the key and ask permission to draw a bucket of water for my use. Often I would be told that the officer was not around, so I would have to wait, sometimes for a whole day. Many times I would return to my room with an empty bucket.

CHAPTER NINE

Main Street

THE RED SOLDIERS had fantastic notions of what an American ate. That's why so many stared in amazement at me while I took my bowl of rice and green vegetables, or my boiled sweet potatoes. They had been told of the huge quantities of canned goods I was supposed to have and of the large quantities of meat I could consume at one sitting. But these soldiers saw no canned goods or meat on my table. The Mastermind and I ate very simply.

Chinese gaolers do not feed their prisoners. So, my problem was to get enough money for my rice and then to get someone who would sell to me. I had still some unhulled rice in a bin downstairs, and I tried several times to sell it and thereby get money to buy my own food. But as usual the officials would give me no help in disposing of it. I finally approached Major Warsaw one day, and in desperation, told him that unless he gave me a permit to sell the unhulled rice and get money for my food I would starve. He said, "You need no permit to sell your property. You may do what you wish with it."

My next problem was to get someone who would brave the stares of the guards and come in to do business with me. Finally, I was able to persuade a very poor man, who had nothing apparently to lose, to take the unhulled rice out on the market and sell it. With that money I was able to purchase a bit of food each market day.

One of the most humiliating experiences of my two years and a half under the Chinese Reds was the twenty minutes I spent each market day hurrying to and from the shops to buy my meager supply of food.

In the first place, it was necessary for me each time to beg—and I mean literally *beg*—the necessary permission from a bitter, arrogant young Communist whose office was in the Sisters' Convent. He would always make me wait and always force me to plead several times before the permission would be granted. He would each time use the occasion to lecture me on my previous excessive eating and on the huge store of goods I had in my quarters. "You may come and search my house," I'd reply, "you will see that there is no food there at all."

Still he would make me wait, and some days, I waited all day only to be told in the end that the permission could not be granted that day. Actually, all that was necessary for him to do was to reach in his drawer and give me a printed pass. Ordinarily, when I came in he would be doing nothing—perhaps reading the paper or a Communist pamphlet, or just talking with one of the soldiers. As soon as he saw me approaching his desk he would say: "You will have to wait a minute." The minute dragged on to an hour, then I would rise again and ask if I might have my permit to go to the market.

"I told you to wait, didn't I?" he'd shout.

Not till now, I told myself, had I known the true meaning of humiliation. I prayed for the virtue that I might accept such unreasonable treatment.

Each market day I trembled in anticipation of having to approach that young man again. And I would kneel and pray for patience to face the ordeal as I should.

Most of the merchants were afraid to be seen doing business with me, and they would refuse to wait on me. Finally, I found an old man with a spark of sympathy in his tender eyes, whose shop was a small stall on the side of the road. He was willing to sell me some rice and vegetables, and he did it quickly enough for me to run back to the mission under the deadline.

The hardest things to endure were the cold unseeing eyes of the people. Why wouldn't they just *look* at me, or nod to me, or give me a smile? I *knew* these people, many I had treated in my dispensary, some of them were my Christians. But they didn't know me now. Why were they so afraid to recognize me? They would look at me and never see me. In the beginning, when I saw a former pagan friend or a Christian approaching me on the road, my face would instinctively light up, and I would begin to speak a greeting, but this cold, distant stare would freeze, unspoken, the words in my throat. The person would pass right by like a perfect stranger, and my heart would be sick.

One day after an hour's pleading with the young officer, I was granted permission to visit a barber to have my long hair cut. Like barbers the world over, this man, who had always been friendly to us, liked to talk, and he couldn't withhold a bit of news from my ear as he clipped my hair in the otherwise empty shop. "Father, you know the order has gone out that no one is to talk to you. You are considered the 'number one enemy' of our government in this part of China."

So this was the reason that no one would speak to me or

recognize me! I consoled myself with the thought that people would never believe this: they knew I was not a criminal. It was merely from fear of reprisal that they passed me by in the streets.

Just before the next customer entered, the barber quickly whispered: "And Ah-Hiu, your cook, is in prison in the county seat at Ping-lo." Poor Ah-Hiu, I thought.

From that time on, each day that I was allowed out to buy my food, I resolved to walk with downcast eyes; I did not want to have anyone placed under suspicion for speaking or nodding to me. However, it was almost impossible to carry out this resolution. The children, goaded on by the soldiers, would shout curses and insults at me: "Vile American devil, American spy—down with American Imperialism." They threw mud and debris at me, and laughed when my clothes became spotted and soiled. Though no adult joined in this, still no one dared to stop the children with the soldiers standing around.

It was a severe test of my patience not to shout at the children, especially when I noticed that some of the youngsters were those who had been often to our mission clinic. Sometimes I was tempted to appeal to the adults passing by, or report to their parents. But I knew that the adults would only turn away their eyes and walk off. So I just gritted my teeth as the stones fell around me. I felt like a social outcast, a leper whom no one would touch.

If only I didn't have to face these cold distant stares! Already on the night before each market day I would find myself getting tense and nervous. Sometimes I would beg the officials to let one of their buyers or cooks purchase my rice and vegetables. They would answer: "Our men are really too busy today to do anything like that for you." The army cooks, some of them ex-Nationalist soldiers, many of them friendly enough, all of them unlettered, would never take the responsibility of buying anything for me without permission from their superiors. However, I shall never forget these Communist army cooks; they were the only ones who would sometimes smile at me; they were the only ones who helped me draw water when I became too weak to do so myself.

I know it was my pride that made me rebel against this twenty-minute ordeal. I tried to force myself to look upon the humiliation in the spirit of Christ. But still I shuddered. I would rather undergo a twenty-minute flogging by the guards, I would rather face twenty hours of questioning by officials in my room, I would rather do anything than face these people I knew, and these children I loved.

One market day as I hurried along to the old man's shop for my rice, a man from a distant village, who obviously did not know what was going on, rushed up to me: "Father, my son is sick, please give me some medicine for him." In former days I usually had carried a medicine kit with me, but not now.

Much as I wished to speak to someone and have someone recognize me, I quickly motioned him to leave me: "No one is permitted to speak to me—go away quickly." I did not even pause in my walking, but after going on a few steps I turned just in time to see three soldiers emerge from a shop and grab the poor, innocent peasant. I heard him protesting vehemently: "I said nothing to the foreigner, I only asked him for medicine. He said nothing to me. . . ." Then the voice faded away in muttered protests. I never saw him again.

That same day, just as I was making my purchases, a group of about ten youngsters rudely ganged-up and seemed more determined than ever to annoy me. My clothes soon became a mess from the mud and refuse hurled at me. Their curses were shockingly disgusting. Two amused soldiers stood nearby, encouraging the children. Then suddenly I saw an old man come out of a shop across the way and angrily disperse the gang of youngsters, rebuking them for their vicious conduct. He was not a Christian, this old man, but in my mind he will always be a Simon of Cyrene who helped me at a moment when I was beginning to feel that in all this great land there was no one to be found to raise a hand or voice in my defense.

I had burned all the available wood in our quarters—bookcases, chairs and boxes, and it was necessary for me now to buy the bundles of twigs that are for sale in every Chinese market place. The bundles weigh only about fifty pounds, but are very unruly when carried on one's shoulders. I had a long bamboo pole such as Chinese coolies use, suspended from their shoulders. For years I had watched peasant women and coolies carry heavy loads in this fashion, little dreaming that one day I would be laboring under a similar burden myself.

The first time I tried to use the pole, amidst the laughter and abuse of the youngsters, I would falter after very few steps and rest. It was a question of weakness and unfamiliarity with the technique. One day the rope suspending one of the bundles snapped and the whole load tumbled to the ground, much to the great amusement of the soldiers and children.

Just then a member of the Youth Corps, which was transporting things from the mission, came along with an empty wheelbarrow on the way back to the mission property. He was a young man of about nineteen, whose sore eye I had taken care of in my room a week before. Certainly he would be kind to me, I thought. I looked longingly at him and then at the wheelbarrow; as he neared me I asked him if he would please allow me to put my firewood in the wheelbarrow and wheel it myself to the mission. He broke my heart with his sharp answer. He said: "No, we have no time," and pushed right past me.

Another time I was struggling with the bundles of firewood and I passed a wheelbarrow standing outside a shop. I asked the owner if I might use it to carry my bundles to the mission. He said: "No, we are not permitted to talk to you."

"You do not have to *talk* to me, just let me use the wheelbarrow," I pleaded.

He shook his head and impatiently motioned for me to leave him.

I began to feel that the youngsters and Youth Corps members were just waiting for my market day appearance on the street. The older children would shout: "Why don't you leave Tungan?" "What do you want around here?" "We do not want you here, you foreign devil, you American imperialistic spy."

I would try occasionally to explain as patiently as I could that my departure was entirely in the hand of the local government.

Others would taunt me about the "death" of the Christian religion. "You will no longer have Christians in China."

"But," I reminded them, "does your government not guarantee 'Freedom of Religion'?"

And they would laugh in ridicule. "You are an American imperialist and your country is the great enemy of the People's Government." Thus it would go on as they followed me down the road. Not satisfied to accompany me to the mission gate, they would stand around outside my quarters and shout over and over again: "Down with the Americans. Throw out the American Devil." This would be followed by a Communist song or two, always punctuated by stones thrown into the room through the already broken windows. I knew it would be useless to shout at them to go away. All I could do was to sit and hope that they would tire soon. I prayed each market day would be a rainy day so that I might be spared some of this ordeal.

But there was an occasional ray of sunshine.

One day a cousin of Sister Louise came along behind me on the way to the market place. My heart jumped to hear the whispered words: "Spiritual Father." It had been months since anyone had thus addressed me. "Spiritual Father, it is a long time since I saw you, you look thin."

I whispered in return, "I am all right. Is every one well in your family?"

"We are well," he said, "but the times are very difficult."

"Be brave; trust to Our Lady. Gold bless you—don't speak any more. It is dangerous for you."

Another day, a member of the women's praesidium of the Legion of Mary passed me. She gave me a quick small sign of recognition with her fingers. And the father of one of our seminarians held his fan to his lips one day as he passed me and whispered. "God bless you, Spiritual Father."

At these moments I would give them a silent blessing and say a silent prayer of thanks to God for the faith they had—a faith, that allowed them to defy the great danger involved in giving me a word of recognition.

While I had eaten rice every day for fourteen years in China, it had never occurred to me to take the trouble to learn how to prepare it properly. The first time I was forced to cook my own rice I instinctively turned to a soldier standing nearby and asked him for some directions. He laughed: "Look," he called to a friend, "here's a man who is supposed to be educated, and he has never learned to cook rice!" I never asked another soldier for cooking aids.

It took several attempts before I could get the rice to come out somewhat as it did when my cook, Ah-Hiu, did it. The sweet potatoes and an occasional egg I could boil without too great a problem—but it took time with the rice. Why, I would say to myself, hadn't I paid more attention during the novitiate cooking courses? Of course, my equipment in the prison room was not the most elaborate, and even if I had learned to bake a cake or make a pie it would have done me little good here without any of the necessary ingredients. I had an old coffee can in which to boil the sweet potatoes, and another can for the rice. Since the soldiers had taken over our kitchen, I prepared my meals under a small lean-to by the side of the rectory. I would place the can on a tiny iron tripod, underneath which smoked the twig fire.

No doubt my vitamin-deficient diet had much to do with my poor health. For several months I had been troubled with dermatitis. My face and hands broke out in a series of sores which annoyed me very much. During the summer I went down with a severe attack of dysentery. I was extremely weak and begged the officials to permit me to go to Kweilin to see a doctor. They laughed at me and said: "We thought you were a doctor yourself, why don't you cure yourself? You claim to have cured other people who were sick."

I said: "Yes, perhaps I did help some sick people, but there is no way now to treat myself since you have taken away my medicine." This brought more sneers.

That fall, as I had feared I might, I had a recurrence of the malaria which had bothered me annually for at least nine years. It seemed more severe than usual, with chills and high fever accompanied, for five days, by the vomiting of a yellow fluid. Again I begged the officials who came in to check on me to permit me to go to another mission in a larger city—but again they merely laughed at me. I begged to have the storeroom opened to see if by chance there might still be some medical supplies left, but no one seemed to know who had the keys. However, I did have a few atabrine tablets hidden in a drawer. I used them and gradually I got over the attack.

Our Maryknoll procurator in Hong-Kong was able two or three times to send money into our section of the interior through a Chinese bank in British Hong-Kong. On these occasions I would get word that the money was waiting for me in a bank in the county seat, but when I asked permission to go for it I was refused. They would tell me that they did not have the power to grant me a permit to leave Tung-an, nor did the soldiers who went back and forth between Tung-an and the county seat "have time." However, almost miraculously, on two occasions some of the money was, for some mysterious reason, brought to me unexpectedly by an official. This money proved to be enough to buy the small amounts of rice and vegetables necessary to stay alive. Without this money, I am sure I would have starved, for no one in Tung-an would give me either food or money—nor would the officials permit me to work for my meals, as they did some of the other prisoners who were less accustomed and able to do manual work than I. Nor did I any longer have saleable objects in my quarters. Everything—bicycles, clothing, bedding—all had been "borrowed".

To keep myself level-headed during these days, I kept praying, rosary after rosary, whenever I was left alone. The Psalms and scripture passages of my breviary began to mean more and more to me as time crept by. In September as the Feast of Mary Mercedes approached, I recalled again that it was to commemorate Our Lady, Ransom of Captives. It was with special fervor that I made the novena as preparation for the Feast. The 24th of September passed and I was still an unransomed captive.

It was during the days following the Feast of Our Lady of Ransom that I felt a violent temptation to make a dash for the British possessions on the coast. But my chances of successfully executing an escape seemed slim when I considered the overwhelming obstacles in the way. To begin with, Tung-an was about 700 miles from the sea. Then I asked myself in whose house I could be sure of a shelter during the daytime; from whom could I hope to get food or money for the long journey? How could I escape the constant searches that went on along the highways and village paths? How could I move at all without a pass? I knew that escape was impossible, yet I found it hard to resign myself to my fate.

I asked the Blessed Mother to forgive me for acting like a spoiled child when she did not secure the longed-for answer to my prayers. After all, I told myself, What claim have *you* on the Blessed Virgin? What have *you* ever done for her? How often have you said her Rosary with careless lack of devotion?

The hours dragged on and the days refused to move. How long can a day be? At this time, because of the Mastermind's presence, I did not reserve the Blessed Sacrament. Then I would ask myself if I would appreciate Our Lord's presence even if I did have it? At these moments—like a man about to drown—I would think of my whole past life, and I knew I had no just cause for complaint.

When I was at my lowest point, Our Lord would send me some small sign to console and encourage me. I recall at this time a girl of the Communist Youth Corps coming to me. I had seen her working as a clerk in the officers' quarters in the Sisters' convent. The Sisters had told me before they left that they thought she was a Catholic from a neighboring mission. Because she was ill, she asked for and received permission from one of the officers to come to me for medicine. The Mastermind was at the market at the time. The guards let her pass—they remained outside, in sight but out of hearing.

When she stood before me she said: "Spiritual Father, I am a Catholic. I want to go to confession."

I almost wept with joy to see the faith of this girl, and I told myself that there must be others on the mission property and in Tung-an and all over China who wanted to talk to a priest again and receive the Sacraments again. The brain washing might not be as thorough as the Reds think. And maybe I was helping such people by staying there, acting as a beacon in the dark.

She told me she was a Christian from Father Regan's mission in Lai-Po and that her father was in prison, that she simply had to take this work or starve. She told me I must pray hard for myself because they were collecting much evidence from the people who were being forced to make accusations against me. "I think they plan a big trial for you, Father. I will pray for you. God protect you, Spiritual Father."

"God protect you," I said.

She went out and I felt stronger and better because of her deep faith.

CHAPTER TEN

Second Novitiate

ONE DAY A high official from the county seat of Ping-Lo came into my quarters and "borrowed" a cot and a few articles from the storeroom. The Mastermind came to me as the officer left and said that he had been ordered to Ping-Lo to attend some meetings there, and that he was turning the key to the storeroom over to the Major. He departed with his big, flea-ridden police dog and from that day, I have never again seen the Mastermind or the police dog.

Now I was alone.

In my solitude, my great consolation was that I was still able to offer the Holy Sacrifice of the Mass. I can never explain why my Mass equipment was not confiscated. I was certain officers had seen the vestments in the attic when I was offering Mass there. Later, after the Mastermind left, when it became too cold in the attic and I brought the vestments downstairs, they saw the articles in my dresser drawer. A few days after I transferred the vestments, the attic door was sealed with strips of paper, and I thanked God that I had rescued the equipment for Mass from that room.

Long before the Reds came into our area, anticipating possible trouble, I had bought a bushel of wheat, a grain we did not grow in our section of China.* I had hidden the wheat in small boxes under the rice bin. But after the Sisters were sent away, my greatest difficulty was in connection with making the altar breads for the Sacrifice of the Mass. I used two stones to grind a bit of the wheat by hand, and sifted out a little flour every two or three weeks. Then I would make the hosts on an iron.

Like so many other things I had taken for granted, I presumed that always there would be others—the Sisters or the catechists—to take care of making hosts for me. All I would have to do would be to offer the Mass. Others would prepare the necessary articles for the ceremony. I had never learned to make hosts myself.

At first, I made a terrible mess of them, and I was very discouraged. It seemed such a simple thing when I watched the Sisters turn them out so beautifully. As I squatted there dejectedly in the smoke of the twig fire, I knew I needed help desperately, and instinctively my thoughts went to St. Martha, whom I always regarded as an expert in matters of cookery. So I begged Martha to help me, and she generously came to my assistance, although it was, I believe, the first time I had ever seriously sought her intercession.

After a bit, the wafers began to come off the iron in one piece and I had a sense of proud achievement as I held them in my hands, round and smooth. Then I would slip them between the pages of my bible and press them flat and crisp.

My baking efforts were a great mystery to the soldiers who

* Hosts could be kept for only three or four weeks without spoiling.

came upon me as I was making the hosts. It had evidently been rumored about that I was getting a bit queer anyhow, and when they would ask me what I was making, I'd say, "Baking cookies for a festive day." I'd used the Chinese expression *kuo tsieh* (to pass a holiday). They would ask me to let them try one of the "cookies", but immediately they would spit out the tasteless, unseasoned, unleavened bread, shake their heads in a pitying gesture and wonder how I could enjoy eating them on a "fiesta." I simply told them, "That's the way I like them", and they would leave the rest of them alone.

By some patient maneuvering I was able to remove the locks from the storeroom door and get out a bottle of Mass wine. It took me three days to perform the trick, using a small piece of iron at rare moments when I was left alone. I saw soldiers look at the small bottle later that day, but they shied clear of it—no doubt feeling that it might be poison. They were searching for guns and radios and other spy weapons. The Mass wine and vestments were of no importance to them, although in other areas I learned that the Youth Corps desecrated the vestments by parading through the streets with them on.

While the Mastermind was living in the room with me, I would rise long before dawn and go to the attic to offer my Mass. There was hardly room to stand erect, but it seemed the safest spot for the Holy Sacrifice. During those days of watching the executions on market days and feeling the pressure of mounting tension due to the continual questionings and threats, it was a great consolation thus to prepare myself spiritually for whatever the day might bring. Needless to say, my Mass each morning was unhurried and devout, for it required no stretch of the imagination to remind myself that each Mass I offered might very well be my last.

Then again I was happy in the thought that even though all

the other priests had been forced to leave this area of China, the Sacrifice of the Mass was to be celebrated each morning here in this spiritual wilderness. I begged courage for all who had been led astray by this new evil.

Now my whole day became a preparation for the next morning's Mass. I would pray that I might not be detected in my pre-dawn hideout in the attic. I wondered about the Mastermind during the four months he was with me. It seemed almost certain that he heard me rise and ascend to the attic—yet he never mentioned it, nor did I. Even the flea-ridden police dog made no stir. One morning, as I had daily feared it might, the inspection of our quarters took place before dawn: I was but halfway through the Holy Sacrifice.

The soldiers downstairs banged on the door with their rifles. I heard them yell, "Open up!" I felt panicky and my heart sank. It seemed an eternity before the Mastermind yelled back, "What do you want so early?" They answered, "We've come for inspection, open up." Then my sleepy, dull-witted personal guard cursed them and said: "Everything is all right, we are still in bed. Come back later and I'll open the door." For these words, despite the curse and the lie, I shall always be grateful to the Mastermind, and as I finished my Mass I asked God to be kind to this Communist. When I came down from the attic, he made no reference to the pre-dawn visit of the soldiers—nor did I. But I saw something decent in this rough young Red soldier that I had never noticed before. On this one point, at least, we understood each other. He would not oppose my worship. After he departed, morning Mass became less of a problem in many ways, and I began to entertain the idea of reserving the Blessed Sacrament. Back a year ago, when Fathers Gilmartin and Nugent were still with me, we did have the Blessed Sacrament hidden and sometimes we would take

It to the Sisters in the storeroom, so that they would be able to adore the Eucharistic Presence. With the guard in the rectory, I did not dare take a chance. However, now that I was alone, perhaps I should.

Then came the doubts—what if the soldiers should discover It in their search? Suppose I was taken away suddenly and did not have time to consume It? Would it be fitting to hide the Blessed Sacrament in miserable surroundings such as these? When I thought of all these difficulties, I would decide that it might be better not to reserve the Blessed Sacrament.

Then the next day I would tell myself that the Blessed Sacrament would be a great consolation to me and I would get strength from the prayers said in Its presence. I could make up now for hours in the past which I might have spent before the Tabernacle, but did not. I told myself, "here in Tung-an, you are alone in all this vast area of southwest China; there are no other priests, there are no other places where Our Eucharistic Lord is being adored. Maybe it is for this reason that you are here in Tung-an, that you may adore our Blessed Lord in the Eucharist."

Thus, for many days I weighed each side of the argument: The good reasons for it and the possible danger of desecration in reserving It.

I decided to reserve It. And as I look back now, it is clear to me that if I had not had the Blessed Sacrament, the constant questionings, the torture of those visits to the market place, the ridicule of the youngsters, the poor diet, the recurring physical ailments would have driven me beyond the point of endurance.

Now, in my aloneness, there were hours in the darkness of evening when I would enter the small room adjoining my quarters and kneel down before the Blessed Sacrament, which was reserved and hidden there in a small cashbox, to pray for China and for my people for whom I could now do nothing else.

The searching parties grew fewer and the youngsters seemed to be getting tired of coming in to annoy me, and as the summer of 1951 became the fall and the fall turned to winter, my visitors became rarer and rarer. Another "Red" Christmas passed with no outward sign of the day's significance visible in Tung-an; if they knew the day's meaning, not one soldier or official came to make mention of the occasion. The order must have gone out making my room "out of bounds." That did not mean, however, that the children did not pester me from the road beneath my window. They continued to stand there, with the approval of the guards, hurling stones at my glassless windows. They would shout out curses and filthy names at me; they would sing their Communist songs; they yelled, "Go home, foreign devil," or "Down with the American spy."

I had one of the four volumes of my breviary and my Bible and it was a comfort to return to them throughout the day. I must confess that for the first time, I recited the words of the breviary with deliberate leisureliness. I relished the Divine Office more than ever before. I made my special prayers the Psalms of David: "I cried to the Lord, when I was in distress and He heard me. . . O Lord, deliver me from the unjust lip, and from the deceitful tongue . . . too long has my soul dwelt with those who hate peace. . . I lift up my eyes to the mountains: whence shall help come to me? My help is from the Lord, who made heaven and earth. . . ." These words of David had new meaning for me here imprisoned in my rectory room. I wondered if there were Reds in David's day when I read: "They have opened a wicked and deceitful tongue against me . . . they have surrounded me with words of hatred and have attacked me without cause... in return for my love, they accuse me... they repaid me evil for good and hatred for love." But David's consolations and his courage and hope became my own: "The Lord watches over thee, the Lord is thy protection at thy right hand... the Lord shall keep thee from all evil: He shall keep thy soul."

The months became a sort of tertianship, as practiced in the Society of Jesus, the "Solitude" of the Sulpician Fathers. This was my opportunity to reflect and appraise things in their proper prospective. Fundamentals became clearer, my own strength was seen as the weakness it really is. I formerly foolishly thought I was too busy for hours of prayer. I now had it forced upon me. In the past, sheer activity often created the illusion of accomplishment; now I was completely inactive. This life of an anchorite wasn't easy for me. My mission life had been a very active one, with much work for refugees, the sick, and the dying. Always there were many mission stations, miles away, to be visited, catechumens to be instructed and baptized. Now I was restless in my enforced idleness. I would tell myself: you are a missioner, ordained to preach Christ in foreign lands. Look at you now, you are wasting your time: no baptisms, no anointings, no preaching.

I would beg the officials again and again to permit me to do some work for the people, to let me reopen my dispensary, take care of the sick, go elsewhere in China to work if they did not wish to let me work here. All of which was greeted as usual with a sneering, "You're to stay here and not do anything for anyone."

I would try to tell myself that it was God's will that I should remain physically inactive, that I might grow strong spiritually. And I would pace my room again and say my beads. I would make novena after novena, especially those preceding the

Feasts of Our Lady. But often it seemed impossible to pray. The loneliness was oppressive, even at those times when I knelt in the blackness before the Blessed Sacrament. No consolation came from my prayers. Often the prayers and the psalms of the breviary I would have to read and reread many times to know what I was reading. Things didn't register so well any more.

During the first three months of 1952, except for a brief period of four days, the Reds did not come in at all to see me; and after many weeks of this, I began to wish that they would come, even if it were only to annoy me or ridicule me. It would be easier than being completely ignored. Not even the guard would answer me or talk to me. Then I recalled that the Maniac had said once that they would abandon me one day and just leave me alone in my room to rot away.

Early in February, some relief for my solitude came one afternoon when two officers entered and started to hammer away on the old theme of my possessing guns. Why had I given guns in the past to the guerrillas? Where did I get them? Where did I have them hidden? Where on the property were they buried? And for the thousandth time, I denied any knowledge of guns and for the thousandth time, I wished they would leave me alone.

But the two persistent officers stayed on and they came back again the next day, and for the next two days. They made another inventory of everything in the storeroom and everything still in my bedroom. They sealed the storeroom with strips of paper and they also sealed up the other rooms. They borrowed a small stove that I used in the cold damp South China winters. I needed that stove when the temperature lowered into the thirties. All these articles, they repeated several times, would be restored—even those that had been "borrowed"—and were merely to be kept, so they might not be lost. They were still "protecting" me.

I breathed a sigh of relief again when they were done with me.

For my solitude I made a daily schedule, and tried seduously to follow it. I would rise before dawn and prepare for my Mass—the only Mass, I would remind myself, to be offered in this whole vast area of Southwest China. Though there was no one privileged to follow the august ceremony, I found myself watching the rubrics of the Mass more closely than ever. How deliberately I now pronounced the words! How reverently I touched the Sacred Host! And my thanksgiving—why hadn't I realized before the value of that time when Christ is literally within me? I thanked God that it was still possible for me to offer Mass—to offer myself to God in union with Christ. Nothing else could have pacified my life and raised it above the degradation and sordidness which surrounded me.

Then, after my Mass, if there was no inspection or visitors, I would prepare a little rice for my late breakfast, after which I would straighten up the room, wash some clothes (if I could get the water from the well), and then I would walk back and forth and say my Rosary, or read a bit of the Bible or my breviary. Then I would make a visit to the Blessed Sacrament.

When I found it impossible to concentrate, I would pace the floor or gaze out the west window overlooking the mission courtyard. I could see the Youth Corps there at their meetings or stare at the soldiers coming and going through the mission gate—acting as though it was their very own military property. Or I would look out the east window at the people slowly going to or coming from the market, or listen to one of the now less frequent accusation meetings on the platform in the field. I felt that I was getting jumpy and nervous and I wondered what was to become of me. What plans did these men have in store for me? Why didn't they come to visit me any more? I'd try to tell myself not to be concerned about my future. I told myself, as I had admonished my Christians so often, I am in the hands of God, He knows I am here. He will strengthen me and watch over me. "Brace yourself," I'd say, "surrender your own will; present your body as a sacrifice living, holy, and pleasing to God."

Still I would find myself getting tense. I'd say if I could only go for a long walk or take a bicycle ride to a neighboring town. If I could only get out of this place for a while. And, I am ashamed to report it, several times I would again entertain the temptation to jump out the window and run down the bus road. When they would yell at me to stop I would keep on running down the bus road, even if they shot at me, I felt.

In the afternoon, about three o'clock, I would start my little twig fire and prepare my evening meal—more rice and vegetables, and an egg if I had been fortunate enough to have one sold to me in the market. From four o'clock until I retired seemed a long stretch then. I would say fifteen decades of the rosary, walking back and forth; and then as it grew dark, I would again go to the little room where I reserved the Blessed Sacrament. I had no oil or lamp now of any kind so my evening intruders were few and far between. I would spend an hour and a half or two hours before the Blessed Sacrament and this seemed not only to console me but to put my mind at rest. A calmness settled upon my whole being: "Come to Me, all you who are weary and I will refresh you." In the quiet darkness there, I would remind myself that my troubles were small compared to those of others. They were as nothing compared to His. I was better able to sleep after my evening period of adoration. Each day I was getting more and more tired as I paced the floor, each night I would drop exhausted on my bed.

Sometimes as I lay on my hard board bed, I would picture myself on the morrow, dying a martyr's death. I would see myself holding aloft my mission cross, giving absolution to my weeping Christians as so many martyrs had done throughout the long glorious history of the Church. It was wishful thinking, full of pride. I would remind myself that my tormentors had not demanded that I deny my faith, or that I step on the crucifix, or sin against any of the virtues. I was convinced that to suffer in such a fashion would be a joy by comparison. I reminded myself of the priests and nuns martyred in north China. That privilege would not be given me; that honor was denied me. No doubt the principal reason was that I was not worthy—these priests and nuns, like the thousands who had won the crown before them, deserved the reward of martyrdom by their holy lives. What had I done to merit such a prize? I would fall asleep telling myself that such a consolation was not for me.

Then the next day it would start all over again, and I would begin another page in the story of utter failure in Tung-an. But my Mass would save me. In those moments I would remind myself that Christ foresaw and foretold and forelived just such a failure as mine years ago. He explained how the grain of wheat must go underground and rot in order to live again and bear fruit. It was the failure of Good Friday, the failure of the Mass. It could be man's greatest hour.

So I would say to myself, "If you can endure this inactivity now, you are a successful missioner. St. Paul's most difficult days were those he spent inactive in chains—not his travels nor his shipwrecks nor his labors for his people."

Still, I was tempted again and again to think of the priestly work I might have been doing had I never left my diocese in

Indiana, where I knew priests were needed so badly. Was it a mistake to have entered Maryknoll and wasted my life here alone in the hills of southwest China among a people who have repaid my efforts to help them with torture more trying than death? Maybe my years at Maryknoll and my fifteen years of labor in south China were all in vain.

Then the thought would come to me that to endure patiently here in my mission prison in Tung-an perhaps was the best possible job I could do for Our Lord for souls. My prayers for my people were from my heart, and maybe Our Blessed Lord would accept them as readily as He would my physical labors for my flock, were I free. I would think that throughout the world there were many others—hundreds of loyal priests and lay people—enduring, far more patiently, far more suffering than I. I knew too, that my people were praying for me and my fellow Maryknollers were praying for me and my friends were praying for me at home, offering their sufferings for me, wanting me to endure and to be strong in enduring.

CHAPTER ELEVEN

The Photograph

IT WAS Wednesday of Passion Week. I was sitting in my room by the east window in the murky, late afternoon watching some stragglers returning from the market. I turned as I heard heavy footsteps coming up the stairs. The door to my room opened and Lt. Leang, a young officer who, I knew, was second in command in the Communist Youth Corps operating out of Tung-an, entered; he was accompanied by a distinguished looking official whom I had seen only once before at the mission. The stranger's heavy, well-tailored black suit told me that he must hold a high office in the Communist Party. No others wore that type of clothes. It was the first time in over two months that anyone had entered my room.

As a formality I invited them to come in and have a chair—which they did.

The year and a half of constant questioning and exposure to their indoctrination, and the sudden months of silence in which I had spoken to no one were having their effect upon me, and I found it very difficult to enter into conversation with them.

But it wasn't necessary for me to say much. Lt. Leang did most of the talking, though as he spoke I found my eyes could not leave the other man, the austere gentleman in black, whose enigmatic smile I was trying to fathom.

"Do you know this gentleman who is here with me?" asked Lt. Leang.

"I have seen the gentleman once or twice here at the headquarters," I replied, "but I have not the pleasure of knowing the gentleman's name."

Lieutenant Leang did not give me the mysterious stranger's name. Instead he began rather solicitously to inquire about my health, which I said was not very good, and about the weather, which I said was never very good to a man who is not free and who is ill.

We had been talking no more than three minutes when from below there came the racket of hurried excited feet. Up the stairs they came and then without knocking a squad of soldiers burst right into the room. The first man was slightly crouched, directing a tommygun at me. One soldier came forward, and smartly saluted the officer in black and handed him a photograph. The rest of the squad of about ten formed a semicircle in front of me.

Mystified, I watched the distinguished looking man in black as he looked tensely at the picture. His strange smile changed instantly and his face became distorted into a vicious expression of hellish hatred and anger. His lips spread tightly across his even teeth and almost without moving his mouth he hissed at me: "Stand up, you." Turning the picture for me to see it he barked: "Do you know who that is?"

It was my ordination picture; the one the suave Mr. Su had taken from the bottom of my trunk during his inspection over a year ago. I answered: "Why, yes, that's my picture. But wait a minute—those insignia, that U.S. medal—how did they get on the picture?"

The man in black, looking at me with contemptuous scorn, shouted: "Is that, or is that not your picture?"

I stammered: "Yes, that's my picture, but those decorations—why that's ridiculous—that big medal is only a toy! No one would put those on a black suit like that. I can explain the whole thing. About a year ago Mr. Su . . ." But that's as far as I got when my accuser barked: "Put up your hands. We know who you are." And with that the soldier nearest me jabbed me with the point of his bayonet because my hands did not go up as quickly as they should have.

With my hands above my head I looked about me at the sinister scene that had so suddenly developed in my prison room. It was so unexpected. It had happened so completely without warning. It was like the climax of tens of schoolboy spy dramas I had witnessed during the Japanese war here in China. I tried to tell myself that this must be part of a play; it was an act. "But *I'm* in this drama," I said to myself. "I'm not a spectator. I'm the villain in this play. It's real."

Then the angry voices with their impulsive charges began to pierce my ears: "You're no priest . . . you are a spy . . . we have all the proof necessary to convict you . . . you are an impostor . . . we know all about you."

"Now wait a minute," I cried. "I can explain this picture. Mr. Su. . . ."

Then the distinguished looking officer in black, the leading man in the drama, stepped toward me. He put his face close to mine and with wasplike anger he shouted: "Are you going to tell us why you came to China? Are you going to tell us who sent you? We know you are not a priest. Tell us all that you know, and it may go easier with you."

And as he stood there in front of me a short fat man took a picture of the man in black confronting me with my hands in the air.

Could they really believe what they were saying? Certainly they must know that I was a priest; that I had labored here for the people of Kwangsi for fifteen years, and that the retouched photograph with the incongruous insignia attached to the clerical garb of my ordination picture was ludicrous. But if it was an act, it was a menacingly realistic one, and the tommyguns and drawn bayonets were all too close and too ominous.

I tried once again to straighten out the situation; but I was ordered to march down the stairs with my hands in the air. On the landing below we paused a moment. The official in black came near me again and commanded me to confess. At that moment the short fat man with the camera went into action again.

I was marched from the rectory past the prisoners in the chapel to the rear wall of the mission property. Lt. Leang was barking out the orders this time and he shouted at me to stand with my back against the wall and keep my hands in the air. The man in black then stepped forward for another picture, after which in a loud voice he again tried to make me confess that I was a U.S. spy. I lost my patience for the moment and I yelled, and, though they attempted to silence me, I wouldn't cease until I had finished my story: "Mr. Su, one of your men took that picture from me over a year ago. At the same time he took that toy medal with the U.S. on it, and he also took the U.S. Army Chaplain insignia. You bring Mr. Su here and he will admit everything just as I am telling you. He knows that the original picture was my graduation picture and that the insignia have been superimposed upon it. Mr. Su said he was taking it to higher officials for inspection to see if I could keep it." I was out of breath, but I felt better after stating my case.

However, the gentleman in black did not seem impressed: "You are lying. We have complete proof that you are not a priest. You admit everything and you may be spared."

"I cannot admit to something that is not true. I am not a spy—I am a priest."

With that, Lt. Leang barked out a command and the two men with tommyguns got down on one knee, and the others with rifles quickly formed a semicircle about fifteen feet in front of me.

Another command from Lt. Leang and the soldiers clicked their guns and leveled them on me.

It was strange. I don't know why it should be that way, but I didn't seem to be afraid, as I had always thought I would be if this situation ever should occur. I wasn't even trembling. I just kept reciting the ejaculation: My Jesus, mercy. My Jesus, mercy.

And then in that brief moment there with my back against my mission wall, and with my eyes looking out into the barrels of the soldiers guns, I felt: now this is the answer to my prayers, the result of my novenas. No, perhaps I didn't want to die just then. But, how much better was this way than rotting in the cold dampness of my prison room. This, I recalled, was what I prayed for—something quick and something private. I'd be spared those thousands of people, most of whom I knew, watching me humiliated; and I'd be spared the frenzied students clamoring for my death. I thanked God that He had made it this easy for me.

I vaguely remember the officer in black abruptly breaking through my thoughts with his shrill: "Well, are you going to confess? We have the complete proof, you know."

But I didn't seem to hear him. I muttered: "What is the

use of my talking; there is nothing further I can say. Only Mr. Su can prove my innocence." And I returned to my silent prayers: My Jesus, mercy.

The officers began again to curse and berate me. The official in the black suit again stuck the ordination picture under my eyes. I was no longer listening or seeing. I closed my eyes and stood straight, indifferent and ready. It seemed an eternity of waiting. But nothing happened. I opened my eyes to see the official in charge angrily walking toward me. Affecting a smile that filled me with disgust, he put his head close to mine; and the short, fat man squatting off to one side took another picture. Lt. Leang barked out another command and the soldiers stood erect and lowered their guns.

I was ordered to march. Actually I felt disappointed that nothing had happened. I felt surprised that I hadn't been frightened. Of course, as I look back now I can see the plan more clearly. I didn't know then that they had no intention of executing me—that I was supposed to be scared into a confession of my guilt of espionage for the United States government. But I didn't become frightened, perhaps because it all happened too quickly, or perhaps because I was happy that those days and months of mental torture were to end—no more questionings, no more sleepless nights, no more trips through those unfriendly, unseeing eyes to and from the market.

I was marched toward the chapel prison. As I walked along between the soldiers with drawn bayonets, suddenly and in desperation the awful thought came to me: the Blessed Sacrament! I had left the Blessed Sacrament in the small room next to my bedroom. I became sick and terrified. Anything could happen to me, but the Blessed Sacrament must not fall into the hands of these evil men who hate Our Lord and His Blessed Mother.

Instinctively, I turned and took a step in the direction of my quarters in the rectory. The soldier nearest me poked me with the butt of his gun and the others closed in tightly around me. Lt. Leang excitedly bellowed out: "Why do you stop? Keep moving!" I started to explain why I had stopped when one of the soldiers shoved me forward.

They led me through the east door of the chapel. The former house of prayer was reeking with a horrible stench, oppressive with the decay of helpless beaten humanity. Not one of those miserable prisoners, weak from illness and lack of food, some of whom I recognized, so much as glanced in my direction; I was just another victim herded in. It was the first time in over a year that I had stepped inside my mission church, and my heart was sick with what I saw. They led me through the battered Communion rail into the desecrated sanctuary, with its ripped out altars and its walls covered with Communist slogans. Where the crucifix used to hang a large picture of Mao Tse-tung smiled down on the misery of the prisoners and on me. They put me finally into the small storeroom on the northwest corner of the chapel.

The eight-foot-square room was empty, the mud floor bare except for two sawhorses with some boards placed across them. These boards were to be my bed. I was still thinking of the Blessed Sacrament left unguarded in my quarters as I was pushed inside and butted again with one of the soldier's guns. "Let me go back to my room just for a moment," I pleaded. "I must get something important there."

They laughed uproariously.

While the man in black watched at the door, and a guard looked through the bars of the storeroom window, Lt. Leang stepped inside to make a thorough search of my person. My belt was removed and taken, as I had seen belts taken from other prisoners; my scapular was ripped off; my rosary, a pocket knife, and even my handkerchief were taken from my pockets. While this was going on the officer in black sneered some insinuating remark about the khaki pants I was wearing.

When they finally finished with me I sat down exhausted on the boards, and I stared up through the small, high-barred window at the murky skies, and the dark, trembling bamboo trees mocking me with low bows in my direction. At this time it must have been about four o'clock. The previous fifteen or twenty minutes seemed a thousand years. I was numb and dismal as death. No one who has been ordered shot and has survived the experience can ever look at the skies and the trees in quite the same way as before. I realized how quickly life could end.

Nothing that had not been rehearsed many times and thought out in detail could have been rolled off by the Reds like the act just performed. Everything clicked. At first I wished that Mr. Su had been there so that he could have proved the truth of my statements about the picture. But then I wondered —if he were here would he have helped me? Obviously Mr. Su must have been the one who framed me from the beginning. Then the whole thing began to clear up in my mind. I could see now Mr. Su dropping the medal and the army insignia into his pocket and putting the picture under his arm. I could see again his queer smile as he left me that day. They had waited until now, over a year later, to produce the picture as evidence. What else had they been planning during these many months? I didn't dare to think. What means will these men not use to attain their evil end? Lies, lies, lies!

About an hour later one of the soldiers came and threw a dirty blanket at me, and I wrapped myself in it, for I was chilled. As I sat on the bare boards I tried to pray; but all I could say was: "Please, Lord, make it as quick as possible. I don't think I can stand a long, drawn-out one."

I remember how, as I sat there in the lowering darkness, with the face of one guard staring through the bars of the window, and the other periodically flashing his light on me through the bars of the upper half of the door, the words of the man in black and Lt. Leang began to echo in my ears: "You are not a priest, you are an impostor." No one had ever said *that* to me before. Often, before they knew me, youngsters had called me "foreign devil." And during the past two years they had called me "American devil," "Imperialist devil," and so on. More recently they had called me "spy," "reactionary," "guerrilla accomplice"—but never a "false priest." Certainly they couldn't believe that. The people of Tung-an would never accept that. These men must have known that I was a priest. Could they possibly believe that I would leave my home in America and spend fifteen years of my life pushing a bicycle over their rough dirt roads, walking exhausted over these endless mountains, standing for hours in my dispensary caring for their ills, eating their strange food, learning their strange language and imitating their strange ways—for a salary from the United States government? They couldn't believe *that!*

Yet I recall how suspicious they sometimes were of me, before they knew me. To so many I was a foreigner and a mystery. I recall students who asked what salary I was getting from America. And I told myself that a life of dedicated charity, of helping others without any hope of recompense, did not make sense to pagan minds. Maybe they could believe that I was a spy in the guise of a priest. Maybe they could accept the idea that a man would do what I had done for a high salary from the American government, unlikely as it seemed.

Or maybe they felt that I would do this for the cause of

Imperialism. Do they not do as much for the cause of Communism? But then why can they not see that I might do the same for Christ and for souls? I could not find the answer there in that damp storeroom prison cell. They seemed convinced that I was not a priest, and the ridiculous, composite picture was the "proof" that I was a spy. It was as if the mother of a child, whom she conceived and nurtured, educated and loved, was suddenly told, after being one with her child for fifteen years, that the child was not hers.

I had anticipated almost every possible charge that could be brought against me, but never that of being a false priest. I had heard of the various charges leveled against other priests, particularly innocent Chinese priests—breaking their vows of poverty and chastity, aiding the anti-Communists—but I had never heard of any of them accused of not being a priest. I could see it clearly now, as I sat dejected and defeated in the gloom of my new cell: once I admitted that I was no priest, it followed as the night the day that I was then a spy for the deadly enemy of the People's Government, America.

Then the thought of the Blessed Sacrament, alone and unguarded in my quarters, returned to torment me. Why was I so presumptuous as to think it would be safe to reserve It in such times as these and in such a place as this? Couldn't I have foreseen that I was taking a serious risk? I must plan some way to return to my quarters in the rectory, for just one minute, even if it were to be the last minute of my life. There seemed no hope, however. My guards insisted that I was never to go back there. I prayed the Rosary on my fingers for forgiveness.

What was next for me? Perhaps they had postponed executing me today so that I could be made a spectacle for the people tomorrow. I was, after all, due to face that mob and be accused in public and ridiculed and humiliated before those people whom I knew and loved; and I was to be executed before their eyes and left to rot there in the field—for I had no one who would come and take me away for burial. No one would dare show so much solicitude for a criminal such as I was. If only I could see another priest for just a moment to confess and make my peace with God, I thought. Maybe they would incarcerate me in a large city, in a prison where there might be a Chinese Father to whom I could talk. The unfriendly young guards never took their eyes off me; they kept staring at me through the bars of the window and the door.

I recall several times turning to the changing guards and asking for a little water. Though I had not eaten since morning I wasn't hungry, but I was very thirsty. Each time my plea was answered by a snarling, "We have no water," or "Wait until later on." I asked several times if I might be permitted outside for a minute to take care of the needs of nature. Again the inhuman answer: "No, you are not allowed to leave your cell." Thus began the infernal stench of my storeroom prison, which became so unbearable as the days wore on that the guards would not show their faces at the window or door without betraying their disgust at the smell that met their olfactory nerves.

Thinking that they were through with me for the night I wrapped the thin, foul blanket around me and lay down on my prison bed.

CHAPTER TWELVE

My Judge

SLEEP THAT NIGHT was no more for me than music for a deaf man. Instinctively I reached for my rosary in the emptiness of my pocket, and I missed it terribly. Leperlike, I felt so completely alone. I sat up on my bed again and saw through the bars of the window the guard still looking in at me, and above his head I could see through the scattering clouds the stars looking in at me also. It was good to see the stars, like friends watching, even though at a great distance. It was not so terribly lonesome when the stars showed that God was looking down on me.

I was reconstructing the terrifying experience of the afternoon's ordeal, when suddenly and unexpectedly the chain on the cell door was loosened and the door was kicked in. About eight soldiers were there, two or three of whom moved inside the room with guns in readiness. "Put your hands up," they shouted, "and come with us."

I made no answer, but started out into the black night, flanked by two soldiers. They took me through the gate that led to the Sisters' Convent, and upstairs to the large room used by the Sisters for their common recreation.

In the rear of the room were two tables, behind which sat the same distinguished man in black, half-smiling, half-sneering, flanked by two lesser officials on either side. On the table was a large Aladdin kerosene lamp without a mantle, burning with a bright, wild flame. I was placed in the center of the room, directly in front of the officer in black, and the guards then took their positions around me.

My hands were tied behind me, and the grim, stern man in the center then took over. Brusque of manner, he snapped: "You know, I'm sure, why you have been brought here tonight?"

I replied: "I have no idea why I have been brought here."

"Now look," he said, "we are giving you another chance to tell us tonight all that you know. In that Catholic doctrine of yours you tell the people to *kao kiai*—to confess. Well, tonight we want *you* to confess, and to beg the pardon of the People's Government. Tell us who it was that sent you here to China. Tell us just what you were expected to do here. *We* know the answers to these questions. We want you simply to confess, and we will try then to arrange for you to leave the country."

"I have committed no crimes, and I have no idea what you are talking about," I insisted.

"You are a spy," he replied.

"I have done nothing against the government of China. I have never mingled in the politics of China, and that is known to the people of Tung-an."

The man in black angrily stood and slowly and with deliberation said to me: "I am your judge, do you understand that? I have been sent here to judge you. We want you to confess to the crimes we know you have committed against the People's

Government of China. Why do you not admit that you are a spy sent here by the imperialist American government?"

As he sat down, one of the officials to the right of the judge spoke up: "We understand that you have made reports to the people here about the war in Korea—is that not so?"

"Perhaps I have mentioned the war in Korea," I answered, "but if I spoke of the war I said only what everyone who read the papers already knew."

The judge, stabbing me with a look of hatred, said: "We have proof that you made derogatory remarks and told many lies about the People's Government and about the Communist Party before we entered this area."

I told the judge that perhaps it was true that I had mentioned events that took place in the North, which all the people of Tung-an spoke of as evil. "But," I added, "this does not in any way mean that I am a spy."

Then there followed a long discussion as to who it was that sent me to Tung-an. (It should be needless to mention that the medium of expression throughout my trials was the Chinese mandarin, or official language.)

"My bishop in Kweilin sent me here," I answered.

"But who sent you to China in the first place?" the judge asked.

"My superior at Maryknoll, New York."

"Yes, that's what we thought," said the judge. "We know about the men this society has in many remote countries of the world, and we know also that you have a Far Eastern Bureau in this society, and that it is used by the American government for espionage purposes."

"That is absolutely ridiculous," I said.

Next the judge asked: "Do you know a man named Mo Ke-sin?"

"I do not know anyone by that name," I answered.

"That is a lie," he shouted, "we have proof that you do."

"If you mean a Chinese priest named Father Ma, I know him," I said.

"I did not say 'Ma'—I said 'Mo' and you know him. Do you know Lai Pei-li?" he said.

"Yes, I know Archbishop Riberi; he is the Pope's representative in China."

Then the secretary on the right of the judge said: "That man Riberi we know is a big American spy."

"How can that be so?" I asked. "Archbishop Riberi is an Italian, not an American."

Because of this question one of the soldiers gave me the back of his hand across my face, and snapped: "Don't answer the officer in that way." This was the first actual violence I had experienced.

The official continued: "Many Europeans are spies for the American imperialists. American money can get anyone to work for them."

There were no more questions for the time being about the Apostolic Delegate or about this man Mo Ke-sin.

I was getting quite weak at this point from lack of food and water, and my mind was almost blank. I started to reel a bit, as in the first stage of anaesthesia. Then one of the soldiers struck me with the butt of his gun and said: "Stand up straight."

I tried to comply and at the same time made repeated aspirations asking Our Lady to help me, to give me the proper answers. Sometimes I would feel that she was near, trying to help me, and at other times that she was far away. Because of my weakened condition I found it very difficult to follow the Northern mandarin language used by the officials. Even in normal times it would be a strain to follow the variations, but now the effort was most fatiguing. Often I would ask the judge to repeat his question. Sometimes I would say that I did not understand his meaning. This would cause him to become very angry.

After one of my interruptions one of the minor officials barked: "It's strange you do not understand the judge's words. We recall when the People's Government first moved to Tung-an you were one of the few people in town who understood the language of the soldiers and officials from the North."

I explained: "That was perhaps to some extent true, because during the war with Japan I met and spoke with many Northern refugees in Kweilin, where I was doing relief work. But now I have become unfamiliar with the Northern dialect because of lack of practice in its use—also it may be because at this time I am very weak and tired. I am not lying when I tell the judge that I do not understand at times."

In my heart there was another reason why I didn't at times understand. My mind from time to time would fly to the little room next to my bedroom and I would think of the Blessed Sacrament there, unguarded through the night. For one fleeting moment I was prompted to say: "Suppose I admit everything, that I am a spy, that I am not a priest—admit anything you say, will you then allow me to go to my room for a minute?" But then, could I trust them to give me the permission after I did confess? It seemed certain that they could not be trusted about anything.

Then, as I tried to answer their ridiculous questions, it seemed impossible not to think that they must realize, too, that the whole thing was preposterous. Still, I reminded myself, they have been saying for years that they would destroy anyone and overthrow any government that opposed them—and they would use any means they thought necessary.

All they wanted me to do was admit that I had carried on

spy activities in Tung-an, and they would forget about the entire case, and expel me from the country. Or maybe they wanted to get rid of me so that the entire church property there would fall into their hands by default. In fact, one of the officials, I recalled, some months before had mentioned how very good some priests in the North were to turn their property over to the People's Government.

They had to save their faces. They knew the "confessions" would mean nothing to me, that I would not mean what I confessed. And I was tempted for a moment to sign the confession and make an end to the interminable questions. After all, I reminded myself, I did say some uncomplimentary things to the people about Communism—just a few minutes ago I had admitted this to the judge. If this was what he meant by carrying on spy activity, then to that extent I was, in their eyes, guilty.

But as I stood there before the big flame of the Aladdin lamp thinking of these things and half listening to the absurd questions of the judge, I came completely to my senses when I heard him say: "You aided the guerrillas by giving medicine to them and curing their wounds."

"I have given medicine to everyone who came to our dispensary," I said, "and I have never questioned a sick man about his political views—no more than about his religious belief."

"But," said the judge, "we have proof that anti-Communist soldiers received medicine from you, and that is a crime against the People's Government, because anyone aiding reactionary forces in any way is guilty of a major crime."

The official at the right of the judge then said with brutal logic: "By your own admission you gave medicine to anyone who came to your dispensary. We have proof that wounded guerrilla soldiers came; therefore you gave medicine to anti-

Communists. So now you might just as well confess to your other crimes also."

I was on the verge of an angry reply when I recalled "the better part of valor," and I hesitated. I said merely: "There are no other crimes to confess."

And so it went, back and forth, they accusing, I denying. My head was splitting and spinning. Dizzily I stood expecting at any moment to topple over. The wild bright flame of the lamp made my eyes smart, and the sinister smile of the judge made everything in the convent room seem evil. Finally I heard one of the officials whisper: "Half the night," or midnight. Shortly after this they untied my arms and led me back to my cell. A corporal in charge of the guards explained to me, with a touch of sympathy in his voice, "If you think over your faults and confess them, I am sure the judge will pardon you." Then he added: "You should not anger the judge by answering him so rudely. You must be careful not to answer back the way you do."

I thanked him for the advice and promised to think it over. I felt nauseated and my dysentery was returning. On my bed, each time I moved the boards would creak, and the guard at the door would throw the beam of his flashlight in my face and ask what I was doing. Every few minutes the flashlight would shine through the bars of the door. I tried to say the Rosary on my fingers, but I found it hard to know whether I had been once or twice or three times around my hand.

Maybe tomorrow there would come an end to the questions and accusations, and I would be permitted to return to my quarters in the rectory and would be able then to take care of the Blessed Sacrament. Too upset to sleep, I tried to recall some of the answers I had made to the questions fired at me.

They seem convinced that I am a deadly enemy, I thought.

I must make it clear to these men that it is the system of Communism, not the people who embrace it, that I do not like. Why is it that they hate me so intensely? They look at me as though anyone not a Communist is not quite human.

Then vaguely I would recall, as I lay there limply in the stench of my cell, what helped to cause their bitter hatred of me. I was not in their eyes a simple Catholic priest who was trying quietly to preach the doctrine of Christ among them. I was a symbol of something they had hated long before Communism raised its ugly head in their land. It was the West they saw in me. The West that had for years humiliated and degraded China—and in my heart I knew these crimes of the Christian West cried for change.

Still unable to drop into unconsciousness, my memory strangely jumped back ten thousand miles and fifteen years. I was a student again at Maryknoll walking along the upper cloister at Rosary time, and I could see the bend of the Hudson River and the Palisades in the distance. And I wondered if I had any thoughts then of this little cell away off here in the Kwangsi mountains, or of the stench of the cell, or the buzz of the mosquitoes raising welts on my face and hands as I lay exposed without a net. Or did I think in those pleasant student days of the mad squeal of rats scampering across a mud floor? And just then a rat ran across my prostrate form, and I sat upright with a sudden jerk, for the one thing that I never liked in China were the rats.

Very early the next morning I was given a basin of water with which to wash my face. As I look back I recall it was the last time I had water with which to wash until three weeks later. Shortly afterwards a soldier came into my cell with a bowl of dry rice and a few spoonfuls of green vegetables. I tried to eat the unappetizing dish, but I had no desire for food. I was parched and begged for a drink of water, and the corporal who had given me the advice the night before brought me a bowl of murky water, obviously the water used for washing their rice. But it refreshed me.

A sergeant came to the door and asked if everything was all right. I told him I was not well, and that I wished very much to go to my quarters for some medicine. But the sergeant merely smiled, and said: "No, that's one thing you cannot do. You are not to return to your house."

All that day a succession of soldiers and Youth Corps members came by to look in on me and utter a few curses at me. Two or three times an official stopped to advise me to think over my crimes, and not obstinately to refuse to confess them. Occasionally, one of the guards would ask if I needed anything. And I would say: "Yes, please get me some water to drink." "All right," he would say, "we'll get some for you later on." It was always "later on."

I kept thinking of the Blessed Sacrament, and I tried to say the Rosary on my fingers—but could never seem to keep the count straight. I knelt on the bed boards and faced the mud walls of the cell and tried to pray. No doubt the sight of me on my knees staring at the wall made the guards feel I was acting queerly, so they came in and ordered me not to kneel. "You may stand or sit, but you are not to kneel, remember that."

Two Youth Corps officials came in to ask questions about my past life, but I was too tired and dejected to answer them. "You have heard the answers to these questions a hundred times, why do you bother me again?" They stamped out, cursing me for my impudence and refusal to cooperate—indignant as though their cause was just. The day seemed like a year. The sun seemed to stand still in the heavens, refusing to go down beyond the hills.

At dusk a soldier came in with a bowl of cold rice and ordered me to eat it quickly. He gave me a bit of water with which to quench my thirst. No sooner had I finished when the two guards commanded me to go with them to the large room on the second floor of the convent where my ordeal of the night before had been held.

The hideous judge in the black suit, whom I shuddered to face again, was sitting behind the desk with the other officials, as on the preceeding evening. The warm bright flame of the Aladdin lamp burned in front of me.

"Well," said the judge, "have you decided to confess your crimes?"

"I have no crimes to confess," I said.

"But you admitted last night that you had spoken against the benevolent rule of the People's Government. We have your confession of that crime," he said.

I said, "The only statements I made to the people about Communism was that they were not to obey laws contrary to the word of God. Perhaps I have spoken against the Communist doctrine of atheism."

"You also admitted that you gave medicine to the anti-Communist guerrilla forces, thereby aiding them," the judge insisted.

"Perhaps in charity I have given medicine to wounded and sick guerrillas," I said.

"*Perhaps,*" sneered the judge. "Why do you repeat the word 'perhaps'? You know it's true." Then with hate and disgust he looked at me, and with awful deliberation he shouted: "Do you know what we can do to you when it is proved that you are a spy for the imperialist Americans?"

"That will be up to you. I do not know," I said.

At this juncture they brought into the room one of my Catholic girls who was about fifteen years old. She began very slowly and nervously to tell her story. She said casually: "Back in 1948 this man formed a women's Legion of Mary here in Tung-an."

The judge then snapped at me: "Do you acknowledge this or not?"

I said, "Yes, I acknowledge it."

The girl went on: "Later he started a Legion of Mary for men, and a branch for teen-age girls."

And I acknowledged this also, not yet comprehending what these remarks were leading to.

She dropped the Legion of Mary and went on to make other insignificant statements, quoting my remarks about Communism at that time. Her testimony was duly recorded by the secretary on the left of the judge. Then she made an insinuating reference to a conversation I was supposed to have carried on with a Christian woman at the mission well. I immediately suspected a frame-up on the sixth commandment. I became quite angry, and my righteous indignation surprised the judge into listening to me. I said: "Don't you think I could have remained in America if I had wanted to do anything like that?"

The judge asked the girl if that matter had anything to do with the Legion of Mary activity, and she said: "No, it did not." He said: "All right, then we shall omit that statement. Go on."

And the fifteen-year-old girl went on. Some of her statements I admitted to be true, others I denied. She was getting quite worked up by this time and seemed encouraged by the interest the officials paid to her words.

She then referred to her brother, whom I had attended when he was very sick three years before. I said it was true that I gave medicine to her brother, but that he was dying with pneumonia when I was called to attend him. She then snapped: "That is a lie. The medicine you gave my brother killed him, and now I am here to get my revenge."

I said: "So that is why you are here to accuse me unjustly." And looking directly at her I asked: "Tell me, you still believe in God, do you not?"

She answered defiantly: "No, I do not."

I shook my head and said: "I feel sorry for you because of what these people have done to you."

Then I looked directly at the judge; he was not moving a muscle. He yelled at the girl to continue with her accusations if she had anything more to say. But she had come to the end of her role. She bowed to the judge, and took a place to one side by the wall.

When the girl had finished, three men were then escorted into the room, and stood to my left in front of the judge. Only one of the three was familiar to me. He was a local businessman who had formerly owned a pony cart, and had done business between Tung-an and the county seat of Ping-lo where Father Herbert Elliott had his mission. He was a good friend of ours, and often brought packages back and forth for us. We called him "The Horseman" and we had been told that he had been killed by the Reds. It was good to see him alive.

He bowed to me and it felt encouraging to see someone whom I knew and who was friendly.

The other two men said that they knew me, but I had never before seen either one so far as I could recall. However, when the name of one was announced I recognized it immediately as the much dreaded leader of the guerrillas in the Tung-an area, who had been captured by the Reds over a year ago. His name was Chin Y-chai. Everyone in Southwest China knew the name Chin Y-chai.

I was greatly surprised to hear this man say that he knew me. The man with him said he had been quartermaster with the guerrillas. He told the judge that he knew me well also.

As they started to narrate their testimony the sickening significance of the whole plot began to dawn on me. They told how I had met with them—"held meetings with us" is the way they put it—and how I had helped to organize and direct the guerrillas in this section.

The whole thing sounded at times so ridiculous to me that I almost smiled. Yet these men seemed in dead earnest, and the possible consequences overwhelmed me. It was almost impossible to answer adequately. The long session with the young girl's accusations had left me limp with fatigue. I couldn't pray. I couldn't think.

The Horseman testified that I had given him a package to be delivered to the quartermaster of the guerrillas, here present, and that he discovered, on turning it over to the quartermaster, that the package contained a revolver and some bullets. At this moment a soldier entered the room and put a large powdered-milk can, wrapped round with adhesive tape, on the table by the Aladdin lamp. My features betrayed the fact that I recognized the object, and the judge smilingly remarked: "So you have seen this package before, haven't you?"

I had to admit that the package was familiar and that it was true that I had given one like it to the Horseman, but I said the package had been sent down from Ping-lo for a man living in Tung-an, whose name was written on the cover. I did not know the man, nor did I know the contents of the package.

The judge sneered: "That's a likely story. You're lying and we know it."

That was all for the Horseman and the two guerrilla leaders. However, the night's ordeal was not yet over; there was a greater shock and a deeper wound yet to come.

I cannot put into words my feelings, when from out of one of the side rooms two soldiers led the closest and most loyal of all my friends, Ah-Hiu, my cook. I could only pray to God that he had not come to accuse me. And while he manifested no sign of friendship his remarks were not at first of the damaging kind. They seemed, at the time, quite indifferent and insignificant.

He did say, I recall, "This man claimed that the Blessed Mother appeared to three children at Fatima." I acknowledged to the judge that I had said that.

Then Ah-Hiu volunteered the information that he had seen me give the milk can to the Horseman. The Catholic girl chimed in with the same observation.

I admitted again that the package had been given by me to this man, but I repeated that I did not know its contents.

The quartermaster stepped forward to say that he had handed the gun I gave him to Chin Y-chai, the guerrilla leader.

Chin Y-chai then came forward to say that with the gun he had killed soldiers of the People's Government Army, and this American spy had directed the activity, he added.

I said: "How could I be responsible for this when I have never seen these two men before, and when I did not know what was in the package?" Often we had sent packages between our missions for the people of Tung-an and Ping-lo. We had done this many times as a favor for the people, never questioning the contents of the packages.

It seemed so utterly useless trying to explain; I was completely exhausted. Repeatedly I had been jabbed by the soldiers at my side—each time I moved my feet or raised my hands to hit a mosquito on my forehead or cheek, they would shout: "Don't move." At first I thought perhaps the Horseman and my cook were there to help me, but they appeared only to pull the noose more tightly. Maybe the package did contain a gun, I thought, and maybe I am the victim of this circumstance and maybe these men do believe that I'm lying. If only this ordeal were being undergone for some doctrine of my Faith! But this political business gave me no consolation and left me with the thought only of its uselessness.

I could see by the watch on the judge's wrist that the hour was past midnight; and shortly after that, my wits dulled as if by drugs, I was led away from the wild bright flame of the lamp into the gloom of my cell. Again the guards took their places by the window and the door, and the flashlight intermittently lit up my face and the room. The mosquitoes took up their buzzing symphony and the rats began their nightlong frolic. And my throat was brick dry from thirst.

I lay down like a man with the pestilence, and tried to recollect what had happened during the past four or five hours, attempting to fathom the significance of the well-performed drama. It seemed I was caught in a mire of quicksand, and help was nowhere to be found. It was the beginning of that stagnation which is slow death. What had I confessed to during those hours? Had I really given that package to the Horseman? I recalled that I had admitted seeing the powdered milk can before. We had used many cans such as that about the mission. Certainly I did not know that any package at any time had contained a revolver. Yet Ah-Hiu seemed to be so certain he had seen me pass that particular milk can to the Horseman.

The charges against me seemed to resolve themselves into some such order as this: I had given medicine to wounded guerrillas; I had formed the Legion of Mary as a spy agency in this area of China; I had passed on to a guerrilla quartermaster, unknown to me, a package containing a revolver; and because of these outlandish accusations I was, therefore, in their eyes not a priest but an American spy. There was in all this fantastic performance at least one consoling thought—maybe I could die for my priesthood since they insisted I deny my holy orders. I could offer my fatigue, which they ignored and my thirst which they refused to satisfy, to Our Lord for my persecuted Christians.

I tried again to pray, but no words came to my lips. Then there was a gap, and I dropped off to sleep.

CHAPTER THIRTEEN

Palm Sunday Matinee

EARLY THE NEXT morning I heard the groans of the prisoners being led out for their brief moment in the mission yard. My head was still spinning and I found it almost impossible to stand erect. I again begged the sergeant of the guards to allow me to return for a minute to my quarters in the rectory. His only answer was: "Confess to your guilt and then it might be arranged."

I answered: "I have committed no crime. If I have offended against any law, it has been done unknowingly."

All that day, fearfully anticipating another session before the sinister smile of the judge, I rested as much as I could, and I prayed that, if it were at all possible, I might not have to go before that man again.

But as dusk settled over the valley of Mutual Peace, parched with thirst and weary with fatigue I was again led to the upper room of the Sisters' Convent. I stopped short in the doorway when I saw standards of the Legion of Mary, and a Rosary on the table in front of the judge.

Seeing my surprise the judge said: "No doubt you know what these things are?"

I said: "Yes, I know. They are the standards of the Legion of Mary."

He said: "You admitted last night that you organized this Legion."

"That is correct," I said. "I started the Legion of Mary in my own mission here in Tung-an."

He handed me a pen: "Write that on this paper."

I wrote it down, and as I handed him back the pen I looked again into his eyes. There was something indescribable there, as though something was working inside him. He was beside himself with hatred when I wrote my admission. And for the first time in my life, I was mortally afraid of a man. There was something preternaturally evil about this one. He put a fear in me that I had never before experienced in my life.

Holding up the Rosary and pointing to the standard with diabolical disdain, he hissed: "Your own Christians have handed over to us this evidence." Then he added, holding a book in his hand: "And we also have this volume to prove that everything we say about the evil of this society is true."

On the front of the manual in large Chinese characters were the words: *Reactionary Technique of the Catholic Church.* And in smaller characters it said: *The Legion of Mary.* Thinking that they were going to say the book had been found in my quarters, I told the judge that it was not mine, that I had never seen the book before. But he said: "This is *our* book. It explains in detail this American spy organization, financed by the American government."

Then he asked for the tenth time: "Now do you still deny you know Mo Ke-sin?"

I still asserted that I did not know him. One of the soldiers at this point walked up to me with a newspaper, on the front page of which was the picture of a man who was definitely not Chinese. I looked closely at it, and recognized a man whom I knew: Father McGrath of the Columban Fathers. The picture was obviously a ridiculous and disgusting composite, showing the unhappy and helpless priest surrounded by five or six lewd women gathered behind a table on which were many pornographic pictures and objects.

The judge sneered: "Well, I see you recognized the man Mo Ke-sin, after all."

I admitted that Father McGrath was known to me, but that I had not recognized him by his Chinese name in the preceding testimony.

Then the judge asked: "Who is the agent who brings you the instructions that come from this man?"

I said: "As it happens I have never had correspondence with Father McGrath. I have received no instructions from him at any time."

The judge then began a long dissertation on the espionage activity of the Legion of Mary in China. Each time I would attempt to interrupt him I would be banged in the ribs or slapped in the face. When the judge pointed to his textbook on the activities of the Legion I shouted out that the book was a lie. "Anyone who knows the Legion understands that it is entirely a spiritual organization, formed to help Catholics in their spiritual life. We do not even discuss politics at our meetings."

Angrily, one of the officials to the right of the judge picked up the Communist textbook on the Legion and shouted: "Listen to this. What is the meaning of this if it has nothing to do with politics and military matters? '*Who is She that cometh forth as the morning star, fair as the moon, bright as the sun, terrible as any army in battle array?'* Is that not part of your Legion's handbook?"

"Yes," I said, "that is the opening prayer, but those words have a spiritual, not a literal meaning."

The man on the judge's left broke in: "Well, who is this Mary, and where is she?"

I started to answer him, but the judge waved his Communist book on the Legion and told me not to bother replying. He motioned the official on his left to be quiet. Then he read some more from the book and paused when he came to the words: *Mary gives to her Legion fullness of faith to conquer the world.*

"How do you explain that?" he sneered. "Does that have a spiritual meaning too?"

I said, "Yes, that also is understood in a spiritual sense, and if you read further you will see that we are to conquer the world with love, and by aiding our neighbor."

Then the judge, banging the desk with his fist, and looking through me with his eyes of hate said: "That is why we must rid our country of this evil spying force in which you are the leader in Southwest China. It is because it is spiritual that we must wipe it out. We can fight the bandits with guns and exterminate them, but this spying Legion of yours we must attack with other weapons."

Puzzled as to how a Communist official could admit to the presence of a "spiritual" force, I interrupted him to ask what evil the members of the Legion had ever committed in China.

But he made no attempt to answer me, except to mutter the worn out communist cliché that all religions are the "opium of the people."

It seemed to me that in their eyes the Legion of Mary was worse than a narcotic acting as an opium for the masses; it was a vital force filling these men with terror and hate. I thought, why won't they come out bluntly and say that they are accusing me of spreading religion which they hate and fear? But they would not give me that satisfaction.

These officials, trained with textbooks originating in Moscow, sincerely felt that religion was harmful to the people. I had seen and heard this many times long before the Reds officially entered our town. Religion is wrong, they were taught, because it insists on the *rights* of the rich—forgetting that Our Lord warned the rich of the way they must use their wealth, and forgetting that the Church condemns profit which comes out of the need of another. Religion is wrong, they learned, because it teaches the *duties* of the poor toward the rich, never having learned the words of the Church about the rights of the poor. And religion is wrong because it instills a spirit of passivity into the people which is inconsistent with the activity vital to complete revolution, thus forgetting that the Church urges patient resignation while working to improve the lot of all mankind, and forgetting also that true Christianity is dynamic action, that a Christian must be apostolic to be worthy of the name.

I was not so unmindful of history as not to realize that in Russia religion at one time had unfortunately been used as an instrument for exploitation and domination. And I was not unmindful of some shameful examples of Christian exploitation in China itself. I could share their just indignation for the base purposes to which some few put the sacred name of religion. The trouble with these men who accused me—and also with their masters in Moscow—is that they took the exceptions for the rule. Because a few had prostituted its sacredness did not make religion an opium for the masses, any more than the wrong use of food by a few could make eating harmful to the masses.

As these thoughts were running through my mind, my eyes were closed. It seemed that everything was beginning to black out. The big flame of the mantle-less Aladdin lamp blinded me; I felt weak and terribly parched; and I prayed they would lead me back to my cell. But it was not yet by any means the end of the evening. Additional "witnesses" were brought in. There were five in this group. I did not know the name of any of them, though two I had seen often in the market place in Tung-an.

One said: "He sent money through me to the guerrillas."

Another said: "I carried messages for him to the guerrillas in the hills."

Too weary to contest the absurd accusations, I merely asked: "Does this involve the Legion of Mary?" When the answer was "No," I'd say: "All right, I did it." Then one man accused me of offering money for the murder of Communist soldiers. I flew in a rage and violently denied I had done this: "I have never spoken to this man before in my life."

The judge stood up and yelled at me to be quiet. He said: "I am your judge, you know. You don't seem to understand that." Then he sneered softly: "We have witnesses here who have very good memories. They can recall your crimes if you cannot."

Another witness said I had called the Communist officials "devils." The judge said: "Is that true, or is it not?"

I said: "Perhaps I did say that when it was the common expression here in Tung-an."

When he used the word devils, I shall never forget how his mouth formed a strange smile, smug and sinister. And I felt a sickness return to my stomach. He didn't seem annoyed that

I should have called him "devil." What was there about these men that seemed so evil?

The man in black repeated the remark: "I am your judge. Keep that in mind. If you have anything to say, speak in a respectful tone."

I said: "You have me here alone, without advocate or friend. I have no one to plead for me, no one to bear witness for me."

At this the man on the right of the judge jumped up and said: "You are guilty of contempt of court. You are not to say such things in the People's Government Court."

The judge barked: "You have all these people to bear witness for you. We know already the truth of their accusations. We want only for you to confess that you are not a priest, and that you have been sent here to carry on espionage for the imperialist Americans."

The man on the right of the judge then told me to write in English that I was guilty of contempt of court. The soldiers released my arms from the tourniquets. It was necessary to wait several minutes before I could hold the pen. But it was a relief to have my arms and hands free. I wrote the words in English and he said. "The sentence for contempt of court is five years imprisonment." It was like adding zeros after a decimal point. I had already been condemned to life imprisonment for aiding the guerrillas!

At least five or six more times that night I signed my name to something they said I did. What these things were I cannot now remember, and my guess is that I did not then understand. I knew that with the signing of each confession I was allowed to sit down and the tourniquets were taken from my arms. But from somewhere strength always came to me to resist the temptation to sit when the testimony concerned my priesthood. I kept repeating to myself: "You are Father Greene, remember that, and you are a priest. Remember also that you cannot get the Legion of Mary in trouble—anything else, admit." So I would say "*Chen-jen*" when the judge asked "Do you acknowledge that or not?" "*Chen-jen,*" I acknowledge it. Occasionally, coming out of a stupor, I would recall that I had acknowledged or signed my name to something that might involve the Legion, and I would ask to have the acknowledgment changed. They would merely sneer at me and tell me again and again that they understood who this woman Mary was and what the Legion of Mary really did, and they were going to use every means in their power to obliterate both from the face of China.

As they led me back to my cell, I asked myself: why do these men hate Our Blessed Mother so? And why do they hate her Legion? My real crime seems to be that I allegedly used the Legionnaires to foster my spy work here in Tung-an. It was ridiculous, yet it was frightening too. And the intense hatred of the judge and his diabolical dislike for Our Lady scared me as nothing before ever had. I was weak, and felt very much alone, and I asked myself if this was what Communism really did to people—the things they feared most they hated most.

The trials went on each night, Wednesday through Saturday. On Palm Sunday about noon I was taken to the Convent, this time to the large hall on the first floor formerly used by the Sisters for the doctrine classes. A group of about sixty people were crowded into the room, many of whom I recognized. A few of them were my own Christians, and one of them was my own cook, standing in the back. Not until the judge came in and remarked to me that the people had come together to testify further against me, did I realize that all this was arranged for me.

The judge and his assistants took their seats behind the long table. The judge then stood up and said he was turning over the trial to the people in the democratic manner of the new People's Government. They were to determine whether or not I had broken the laws of China. Turning to me he said: "You will see what these *lao-peh-hsing* (ordinary people), some of whom were members of the reactionary Catholic Church, think of you."

Sitting in the front row was a rough, disheveled looking young woman, unknown to me, smoking a cigarette. A feeling of sickening disgust went through me as I saw that she wanted to have the floor. I prayed to God to spare me from what I feared certain was to come. Don't, I pleaded with Our Lady, don't, before these people whom I know, let them frame me on any charge against purity, as they have done to other priests.

I was relieved to hear a man's voice open the meeting by shouting out a few of what now had become routine accusations. I didn't bother to listen to him. I was telling myself: "Now, remember you are a priest. No matter what is said here you cannot deny your priesthood before these people—nor are you to implicate the Legion of Mary in any way."

Next stepped up the young girl who had appeared against me on the second night of the private trial. She repeated in detail my association with the Legion of Mary. Then other witnesses took their turn, recalling the place and the day, and in many cases the hour even of the day on which I had made statements derogatory to Communism, three or four years before. I could not resist the temptation to remark to the judge: "What marvelous memories they have." He snarled: "You are to make no comments about the witnesses nor their memories."

At this point the disheveled young woman in the front row from whom I had anticipated a bad time, finally was recognized by the judge. But instead of the accusation I had feared, she yelled that in our dispensary I had blinded her child. I said firmly: "I do not know this woman. I have never seen her in our dispensary." She rushed up to me like a person mentally deranged, clawed my face and wildly pulled my hair. One of the soldiers pulled her away and she sat down. I was greatly relieved.

Another man whom I didn't know accused me of having guns, which, he maintained, he had seen in my house. A woman got up and said she had worked for me and received no wages. I told the judge that she was never employed at the mission and that, furthermore, I had never seen her before. He told me to keep my eyes down and be quiet. Some merchants claimed, without very much conviction in their voices, that I owed them money. However, as the accusations piled up and my energy waned, gradually I found myself saying "Yes," and "I acknowledge it," to statements I did not understand. I said to myself: "Certainly, these people cannot be sincere. They must know they are lying." So I would answer their accusations: "Yes, I acknowledge," or "That is what the witness maintains," or "What can I say to deny it?" I could sense that some spoke in fear, some were trying to be angry, but others as they came up and struck me and spat upon me obviously were serious in their hatred.

And now it was Ah-Hiu's, my cook's, turn. Several times I had looked back at him standing in the rear of the room, but each time he would turn away his eyes and refuse to look at me. At a sign from the judge he came rushing eagerly and angrily toward the front where I was standing. Never have I seen in such a short time so marked a change come over a man. His drawn face was flushed with hatred. He looked at me and called me by my Chinese name without the title Spiritual Father: "Chin Peh-teh," he said. "I will prove to all these people that you are no priest and that you have broken all the commandments of God."

I could hardly believe my ears as he went down the list of God's laws, emphasizing his accusation by slapping my face after each commandment, and poking his finger into my cheek with each accusation. "This man, who says he is a priest, but who really is no priest but a spy, has broken the First Commandment, for I who have lived with him have never seen him pray. He has broken the Second Commandment by repeatedly using the name of God in vain and by cursing the Chinese people. He has broken the Third Commandment by refusing to say Mass on Sunday and by working on that day. He has broken the Fourth Commandment by disobeying his parents and by refusing to return to the bedside of his dying mother. In his dispensary he has given poison to kill people; he has ordered the murder of soldiers of the People's Army, and thereby he has broken the Fifth Commandment."

He hardly seemed to pause for breath but kept piling up eloquently the horrible list of my crimes. I wondered what he would say about the Sixth Commandment, and was relieved when he said merely: "He has broken the Sixth Commandment by his impure desires, obvious from the fact that he always gave Holy Communion on Sundays on the women's side." He said I had cheated people and given insufficient wages to those who worked for me. I had told ten thousand lies about officials of the People's Government. I had had bad thoughts and covetous desires.

When he finished the list of commandments, in a fit of uncontrollable anger he struck me flush on the mouth, and yelled at me to kneel down. Without realizing what I was doing I got down on my knees. When I realized what I had done I rose, but he struck me again and forced me to my knees. In a loud, fierce voice he yelled: "This American Devil for years has given me a narcotic in the form of medicine to force me to work for him and to be loyal to him and his false cause. With this drug he has made a slave of me. And now before the People's Court I testify that he is no priest but a spying imperialist devil." His mouth was frothing and his face burned with the fire of hatred. Then he turned to me and hissed in my face: "Chin Peh-teh, I am no longer the old Ah-Hiu that you knew."

From my kneeling posture I looked up into his eyes and slowly shaking my head I said sadly and deliberately: "That is very true, Ah-Hiu, you are not the man I once knew and loved." With that he struck me again with the back of his hand on the mouth.

The judge broke in at this point and smilingly said to me: "You see, we have nothing to do with this. These are your own people who thus accuse and strike you."

I wondered as I knelt there what diabolical thing had got into the heart of my once loyal friend Ah-Hiu. I asked God to forgive Ah-Hiu, for I knew something had happened to him, and he was not guilty of what he was now doing. What had Ah-Hiu undergone during those five months imprisonment in the county jail? There was an obvious *physical* change in him, but that was nothing compared to the change in his mind. From a loyal, zealous follower of Christ he had changed to a bestial hater of all that the Church stood for. I tried with a look of pity to let him see that what he had been told concerning me was not true, and that I still felt the same toward him. I looked at him and said: "Ah-Hiu, never have I done anything or said anything to harm you. Do not believe the lies you have been told."

Again he struck me and said: "You have broken all the laws of God and you have tried with dope to make me your slave."

Then he added: "In those famous Legion of Mary meetings you told us it was a glorious thing to die for Mary."

I said loudly: "It *is* a glorious thing to die for Our Blessed Mother."

Ah-Hiu hit me in the mouth for that, and shouted: "We have only one savior, Mao Tse-tung." He pointed to the large picture of Mao and said: "There is our savior."

My heart sank like a piece of metal in the ocean of my despair. I had hoped that he had been able still to keep his faith. What he thought of me didn't much matter so long as he did not deny Our Blessed Lord and Our Lady. But now those soul-poisoning words: "Mao Tse-tung is our savior."

As Ah-Hiu, panting with rage, walked back to his place in the rear of the room I rose from my knees and looked at my judge. He repeated: "This is not our doing. These witnesses are your own people of Tung-an, some of them your Christians. This testifying is their own wish—we have nothing to do with it." And he and the other officials laughed loudly. Then he asked me to make a statement now that the day's testimony was over.

I was lifeless with exhaustion and merely stammered some remarks to the effect that the people of Tung-an knew that I had tried to help them for these many years, and that they knew I would not in any way harm them. Then I said: "Perhaps I did say that the destruction of the Christian Church in the North was diabolical. Perhaps in charity I did give medicine to the sick guerrilla soldiers, but it must be obvious to the people of Tung-an that my actions were in no way done as a work of espionage. I repeat that I am a priest and not a spy."

The judge then rose and asked the people what further should be done. They shouted: "Make the American Devil confess all his crimes." The woman in the front row with the disheveled hair shouted out: "He has not yet made an admission of his guilt."

The judge said: "What do you wish done with this man?"

They cried out again: "Make him confess."

The judge said: "And if he will not confess?"

"Kill him, kill him."

No one seemed to miss his cue. The responses were shouted out with enthusiasm, like the applause of a radio audience breaking forth automatically at the signal from the announcer.

I was led away limp and listless to my cell. By the position of the dying sun I could see that the ordeal must have consumed more than five hours. A guard came in and handed me a bowl of rice with a spoonful of green vegetables on top. I could not swallow it. He gave me also a little warm water in a small cup which I drank with one gulp, but which failed in any degree to quench my parched palate.

In my semi-delirium, Ah-Hiu seemed to be still standing in front of me. "Mao Tse-tung is our savior." I buried my head in my hands to shut out the vision.

CHAPTER FOURTEEN

My Matchstick Rosary

IT DID NOT seem possible that the officials would demand anything more of me on that Palm Sunday in 1952. I felt sure that the public accusation had been arranged as a special matinee to take the place of the usual night "trial." So it was with at least that thought to ease my exhausted mind that I lay down to rest. But in the twilight of that Sunday my cell door was opened and the guards, with a ring of devilish glee in their voices, ordered me to get up and to go with them to the upper room in the convent. It didn't seem physically possible that I could bear to enter that evil-infested chamber again.

That night the chief witnesses again were the two ex-guerrilla officers, and the Horseman. Although it was obvious that they had no personal knowledge of the Legion of Mary, the judge with subtle insistence tried to connect their testimony with the Legion. A few local men who had not been at the afternoon session were on hand to say vehemently that I had coerced them to enlist with the guerrilla forces. It was clear that these men were accused criminals themselves and were testifying against me in the hope that they might thereby be exonerated. I hopelessly denied the fantastic accusations, and asked the judge how he could believe such a charge, and how he could possibly link these lies with the activity of the Legion of Mary.

I refused to acknowledge again or even reply to the charge that I had given money to the guerrilla quartermaster with instructions to kill certain Communist soldiers who were stationed on the mission property. The quartermaster said that for each soldier of the People's Government killed by the guerrillas I "offered the sum of sixty dollars in United States currency." I looked at the man and said: "You know that your charge is a lie."

The judge angrily rose from his chair and started around the table toward me, and I was preparing for a blow from his fist. With my hands this time bound tightly with rope behind my back, it would have been impossible to ward off his assault. But instead of striking me, he uttered some curses, and stuck under my eyes a page of his law book which, he said, told how a criminal should conduct himself in the presence of his judge. Then he told the soldiers to release my arms so I could sign a statement admitting that I was guilty for the second time of contempt of court. I signed the contempt charge, realizing that I had now been sentenced to life imprisonment, plus ten years!

I did not see Ah-Hiu Palm Sunday night until he stepped out of one of the small rooms. He was calmer now than in the afternoon. He came before the judge and, without preliminary remarks, he made this accusation: "You recall," he said to me angrily, "the day you threw a soldier of the People's Government out of the kitchen?" Then turning to the judge he added:

"I remember how this American spy not only insulted that innocent soldier, but he ordered one of his hirelings to kill him with a knife."

I was too weary any longer to attempt to deny or explain. I simply said: "The whole story is fantastic."

Ah-Hiu wished to continue, but the quartermaster interrupted to say that he recalled the very day on which the transaction took place. He insisted that he was present and had heard everything that was said at that time.

I muttered something to the effect that since everyone seemed so certain of it, what could I say?

The judge snarled at me: "It is strange that *you* cannot remember. These men recall the details so vividly. Obviously you are lying."

My mind was incapable of reflection, but the thought kept vaguely presenting itself to me that possibly my cook and these other men were to be punished for the various crimes of which they accused me if I should be freed. I stood wearily through the haggling for what seemed an interminably long time. At that weird and weary hour all I was interested in was reaching the end of this interminable Palm Sunday. When finally they returned me to my cell I let myself drop with a lifeless thud on the boards and passed immediately into unconsciousness.

But it was still dark when I awoke. I felt a painful twitching in my right leg. As I rubbed the circulation back, I began slowly to recollect parts of what had transpired the night before. The story of the Communist soldier whom, according to Ah-Hiu's testimony, I had caused to be stabbed with the knife, came back to my mind. I remembered there in the darkness of my foul cell the actual event as it had taken place about two years before. The soldier had accidentally cut his hand in our kitchen and Ah-Hiu had run for me to come and attend the man. Why had I said last night, as the judge asserts I did, that I had ordered someone to knife the Communist soldier?

I called the guard and started to explain to him that I did not understand what I was doing last night when I admitted committing a crime that I had never done. He said: "Don't bother me with that nonsense. All you are supposed to do is think over all your crimes and confess them."

On Monday evening of Holy Week, as had happened on two or three of the previous nights, the soldiers put my arms in tourniquets. They pulled the rope tightly and my shoulders were held back in a painfully awkward position. I could just see the backs of my hands hanging high and limp at the level of my chest. After a while a large white ring appeared on the back of each hand, and a red spot in the middle of each white ring. At first there was considerable needlelike pain shooting through both limbs, and then they became numb. Later that night as I looked at the backs of my hands, devoid of feeling and hanging by my chest, I would think: "This can't be happening to me." It was as if I were standing over at one side of the room, looking at this figure with the tourniquets, upright before the bright lamp and the judge in black. It was like watching a movie. I could see myself as if in the picture—and then suddenly I'd realize that it wasn't a picture, that it was real. Then I'd mumble to the judge: "Look at my hands, they have no feeling in them."

Utterly without the least touch of human compassion, he cursed me and told me to pay attention to the witnesses and to the court. It seemed unbelievable when he ordered the soldiers to apply the tourniquet more tightly because of my misconduct before the court.

I recall that more angry words were directed at me, but I

don't think I could any longer follow their meaning. Then it seemed that everything gradually went black, and I went down in a heap on the floor. A soldier must have picked me up, for when I came to I was sitting in a chair. This, far from eliciting a bit of pity from the heartless judge, merely angered him the more. Cursing me, he said: "You American spies think you are such good actors. But even as spies you are not so good."

I was about to tell him for the one hundredth time that I was not a spy, when he surprised me by asking if I had ever heard of the German Gestapo. I told him that I knew a little about it. He explained that while they were ruthless and efficient, they could not compare with the Russian Secret Police; they are the best, he said, pointing with his hand high over his head. Then he said disdainfully, "You Americans, you are way down here." And he gestured toward the ground.

I felt no urge to comment. What would be the use? They would merely laugh at me, or get more angry with me. I merely nodded and let it go at that. The only thing I must not do, I knew, was to deny my priesthood, nor must I involve the Legion of Mary in any of my confessions, no matter how often they accused me or tormented me. I reminded myself that other priests were no doubt having far worse torments than I. Perhaps this ordeal of mine, all these misunderstandings and lies could be endured for them as well as for my Christians. I prayed the *Memorare* for strength.

That night, as on several previous nights, the guards very seriously warned me not to attempt to jump from the upper balcony of the Sisters' Convent as we walked out of the large room. Many times recently the soldiers had made remarks intimating that they thought I might be thinking of suicide. Each time I told them: "Have no fear. I would not take my own life." Perhaps I shall never know whether they were afraid I might commit suicide or whether they were trying to put the idea in my upset and weary mind. It seems now unthinkable that such thoughts ever entered my head, yet I know there were in those dreadful days many long gaps during which I could recall nothing I said or did.

During the half-waking, half-delirious hours of the painfully long days I would try to remove from my mind the sinister look of the inhuman judge, and the evil intentions of all those who had come together against me. For some small comfort I would try to pray. I would try to say the Rosary on my fingers. The prayers came hard and distractedly. It was impossible to keep count of the number of prayers I said. Then for the first time I noticed five or six burnt safety matches lying in one of the foul corners of my cell. I picked up the matchsticks and broke each one in half, making ten pieces about an inch long. I placed them in a row on the board bed, and I squatted in front of the matches and started slowly to say the Hail Marys of the Rosary. After each prayer I would move a matchstick about two inches to the left, then go on to the next prayer. When I had completed one decade, I would move them back to the right again one by one as I said my Aves.

For each decade of the Rosary I would pray for a special intention: that my mind might remain clear; that my body might remain strong; that my dysentery might clear up; that the infection in my ear might get better; that my Christians might remain faithful; that Ah-Hiu might regain his mind and his faith. I felt stronger after these moments of prayer. And at such moments of respite my mind would go back to the disturbing fact of the Blessed Sacrament lying in my quarters.

As I prayed I had not noticed the surly guards at the window and the door gazing at me in wonderment. No doubt about it, the sight of me squatting there on the boards staring at broken bits of burnt matches and moving them occasionally from side to side must have convinced these men that I had reached an advanced stage of dementia praecox. However, according to their plans I was apparently somewhat ahead of schedule—they had still some more use for me, and they sounded rather anxious as they shouted out: "What are you doing there with those sticks?"

"Thinking," I replied slowly, "just thinking."

And otherwise I would ignore them.

I didn't know, until the end, that the guards had informed the judge about this queer thing they had seen me doing in my cell. When the officials heard about my inexplicable match-stick moving they were certain that I was very close to losing my mind. So anxious were they about that possibility that for the next three nights the judge and the officials were rather lenient to me. I have no doubt that those men, at least the shrewd judge, realized just how far the mind could be taken before it crossed the line from sanity to insanity. My judge and his team of officials knew the system well. As I observe it now, it is the same detailed procedure followed in each trial for each victim of the Reds, whether the victim is in China or in Europe.

In fact the judge mentioned one evening that he understood the nature of my replies since he had conducted many similar "trials" of foreign spies before. He also boasted of his knowledge of the Russian language, and spoke of the close friends he had in the famed Russian Secret Police.

In the comparatively mild meeting of the Tuesday evening in Holy Week there was much mention of the cell workings of the Legion of Mary. At one time during this discussion the judge pointed his menacing finger at me and his face looked unearthly as he stared out from the wild flame of the kerosene lamp. He said: "We are not concerned any longer about you —we want to know now who it is that directs your espionage activity here in Southwest China. We want you to tell us what your connections are with the imperialist agents Riberi and McGrath."

Then I began to wonder if my trials were being held in order to get evidence against Archbishop Riberi and Father McGrath. I did not know at that time that Archbishop Riberi had already been expelled from China. Nor did I know then the widespread hatred the Reds have for Our Lady throughout China. I could not, and still cannot, explain to myself the reason for their hatred. There is no question about it, the Legion of Mary is bearing, and has born, the brunt of the persecution against the Church in China these several years. No Communist I ever met could give me any reason for his intense hatred of the Mother of God, but he felt it.

I tried to recall as I moved my matchstick Rosary back and forth along the board bed, if ever in the long history of the Church men had hated and attacked the Mother of Our Lord as these men do today. They have, however, blindly chosen for the object of their diabolical assault the one target they cannot in any way harm—the one target that will in the end prove their undoing. I found my mind going back to the Book of Genesis: *I will put enmities between thee and the Woman, and thy seed and her seed,* and *She shall crush the head of the serpent.*

I recall that one of the officials, the man with the thin voice, came forward toward me once as I stood there before the judge, my arms bound with tourniquets, and he sneered: "Your God got you into this. Now let us see Him get you out."

The judge and the others laughed loudly at this clever piece of sophistry.

That night at a signal from the judge a soldier came forward with a folded paper which he opened up on the table by the Aladdin lamp, and then he stepped back to his original position. I could see that the document was a large map of China, but that particular map was in no way familiar to me. I was certain I had never seen it before.

The guerrilla quartermaster spoke up: "This American spy gave us this map through one of his agents in the Legion of Mary."

The judge asked: "Do you acknowledge this or not?"

I answered: "I have never seen this map before." And looking more closely at it I noticed that the names on it were in the French language. I said to the judge, rather elated with my discovery: "This map is in the French language. What would I, an American, be doing with a map of China in French when there are plenty of maps of China available in English?"

The judge seemed quite disturbed at this revelation—for obviously he knew neither English nor French—and he glared in anger at the young official to his left, the man apparently who had concocted this piece of evidence in the first place.

But, of all people, it was my former cook Ah-Hiu who came to the aid of the slightly embarrassed judge. My cook said with definite conviction: "I can testify that I saw this map on the bookshelf in this man's room. It was on the bookshelf by his bed, and sometimes he would take it out at night to study it."

It was "this man" whenever Ah-Hiu referred to me now. Never, since the day he had been taken away from the mission by the Reds did he call me "Spiritual Father." It was "this spy" or "this devil" or my Chinese name "Chin Peh-teh."

His word was enough. It was all the evidence necessary to prove that I had maps of China illegally in my possession. (A Communist could not conceive of anyone possessing a map for any other reason except espionage.) And that crime, too, was duly recorded in the testimony by the official on the judge's right.

For some time I kept insisting that I had never seen the map before and I refused to sign a statement confessing that I had possessed it. Still, as the questions piled up and Ah-Hiu came forward time and again to state his evidence, I began to waver. Ah-Hiu was so certain. He even remembered the very shelf in the bookcase where the map was kept. I began to wonder if perhaps one of the other Fathers might not have had the map and that I had never noticed it. As time wore on and I wore out, I signed a confession not only that I had possessed the map, but that I had passed it on to the guerrilla quartermaster just as he said I did. At that time it didn't seem important enough to argue about it in the face of statements that were accepted without question. It wasn't until after the confession was read back to me that I realized that the confession included the transfer of the map through a Legion of Mary member to the guerrillas. When I heard that I denied the confession. But the judge merely laughed and said, "Once the confession has been signed the matter is closed."

When the map evidence was finished I turned and saw four of my Christians being ushered into the wild bright light. Each one of these obviously frightened men timidly made a single statement.

One said: "This man claimed that the Holy Mother appeared at Fatima to three children."

Another said: "This man told us it was a glorious thing to die for the Holy Mother."

The third said: "This man said the people should not pay taxes to the Communist officials."

And the fourth said: "This man said that Communism is the opium of the people."

When the four men finished the soldiers were ordered to remove my arms from the tourniquet. Then the secretary on the right of the judge slowly read the first accusation and the judge asked me if I admitted the charge. I said: "The statement is correct. I did say the Blessed Mother appeared at Fatima." And I signed a confession acknowledging that the second accusation was true—not realizing that to die for Mary meant, in the eyes of these men, fighting for the guerrillas against the People's Government.

The other two statements were read, and I confessed that they were in part true. I was given no opportunity to explain why we had in the beginning told the people not to pay the taxes. Nor would he give me time to show how Communism —not religion—drugs the people.

Very abruptly the judge shouted at me: "Do you know that we have learned that you have the rank of colonel in the American army?"

I said merely: "Ridiculous." But I thought it rather good of them to determine that I had such a high rank!

Then he added with a note of glee in his satanic voice: "But we also know that you are now in disgrace with the American army for making a failure of your espionage assignment here in Southwest China."

It seemed incredible that these otherwise intelligent men could possibly accept the fantastic idea that I was a military man; yet they were not smiling but bitterly in earnest when they spoke. That they believed it seemed all the more evident when the official with the thin voice asked: "Why are you making this sacrifice of your life for the imperialist American government, when they will not so much as raise a finger to help you?"

I said: "What I have done here in China has been done for God and for souls—not for the American government."

The judge sneered bitterly: "We know that in former years the armies of the imperialist West came to our land and killed our people because of the teachers of your Christian religion. But today they would not dare. The strong People's Government and our invincible army are no longer insulted by the West."

After a pause to let his eloquent words penetrate my weary mind, the judge asked: "Did your God send you here?"

I said: "Yes, He did, through my superiors."

The judge was red with anger, and he shouted out: "If you say the Catholic Church sent you here to do what you have done we will wipe every sign of it from the land of China!"

I berated myself again for having made a statement that might cause more trouble for the Church and for our Christians in China. I tried to explain to the judge that my superiors in the Catholic Church sent me to preach religion only; any laws that they claimed I had broken had nothing to do with the Church or my society or my bishop.

About this time I became possessed of the conviction of the definite evil in the eyes of this judge. Something seemed to come forth from him that made me feel like ducking my head so as to avoid it. Then he said viciously: "Do you know what we will do to you if you do not confess? We'll throw you back in that cell of yours and forget about you for a few days—and you'll go mad." He didn't say that I would die there, he didn't use the term to rot away, he hissed the words: "Go mad."

I managed enough strength to repeat: "You are free to do

what you wish. I cannot admit to crimes which I did not commit, nor can I deny that I am a priest." I used the words "Spiritual Father" and the judge looked at the official on his right and repeated the words mockingly: "Spiritual Father."

He ordered the soldiers to remove the tourniquets, and carrying a large number of folders he came around in front of the table and began to pace up and down beside me. He laughed: "You see this pile of papers, this evidence, all these confessions that you have signed. We are not going to lose these; and the witnesses that appeared against you, they're not going to die overnight. Whatever you may say is of no weight against all these."

I said: "I do not know what confessions I may have made, but I want it understood now that I did not commit any crimes against God nor against the people of China whom I love. I call God to be witness to what I am now saying."

The judge smiled and taunted me: "Let us see your God get you out of your predicament now."

I said: "You would not understand."

And that was all for that night.

The next day I just sat in my cell and moved the ten pieces of burnt matches to the left and then back again to the right, and said my Aves.

Several times the corporal came to the door of my cell. I sensed from the look in his eyes and the tone of his words that he had just a little pity for me. Because of the stench of my cell and the filth of the floor he brought me a small pail of ashes to sprinkle about to absorb some of the excrement. Once or twice, when I was brick dry with thirst, he alone had brought me a bowl of warm water to drink. Perhaps the other guards also would have done the same, but feared their solicitude might be detected by one of the officials. I do know that they maintained their surly bitterness toward me to the end. It was the corporal who seemed to notice me holding my splitting head, and I'm sure he was sincere when he said: "Look, don't be afraid to confess your crimes. Our great leader, Mao, is most merciful and he will pardon you if you will only repent. Tonight tell the judge everything, and your bitterness will be all over."

I said: "I'm afraid you do not understand."

Shaking his head the corporal moved away from the door and left me alone. Still, of all the men with whom I came in contact during those many months of difficult days and nights, this corporal was the only one who dared to manifest even a slight concern for my welfare. "And this man was a Samaritan," as with the man in the gospel who fell among thieves. He belonged to another camp.

Since I had no desire for food, and since the cold rice nauseated me, the temptation again grew strong to make no effort to eat, and in that way hasten the end. It was sinful to entertain the notion, and I asked God to have mercy on me.

It had become difficult for me now to recall the day of the week. I was sure of Palm Sunday, and then I began to put scratches on the wall for each day. There were three marks now; but I wasn't certain whether or not I had missed a day —or possibly two. I asked the corporal and he said: "It is the third day of the week."

I knew then that it was Wednesday of Holy Week.

CHAPTER FIFTEEN

The Judge's History Lecture

WHEN I MENTION my physical pains or my mental anguish, it is done not to elicit sympathy for myself, but rather that you may in some way better understand the horror and the inhumanity of the Communist system which confronts us, and that you may more fervently pray for the Christian men and women who are at the moment enmeshed in it.

Repeatedly on Wednesday I begged the guards for a bit of water. My lips were adhering to my teeth. There was a thick, sticky film over the inside of my mouth, and my tongue seemed twice its normal size, making it very difficult for me to speak. The corporal had not been around all day, and the other guards merely laughed when I requested something to relieve my thirst. Once or twice they deliberately sipped tea at my cell door.

I recall sitting in a sort of daze on the edge of my board bed, holding my fingers before my eyes, staring at them. Each time I returned to consciousness, I found myself gaping at my fingers. The day was interminable, my headache was unbearable. Should I be called before the judge that night, I would make it clear to him and the other officials, that in the eyes of God I felt I was innocent of any crime, and that was all that mattered. What they falsely accused me of doing would not make me guilty in the sight of my Eternal Judge. There in my cell sometimes it was easy for me to think of statements I would make or answers I should give. But it seemed to me that the proper words never came to me when I was before the judge.

Fortunately, that evening I had no appetite for food, for if I had, there would have been no means available to satisfy it. The guards opened the cell door and ordered me to go with them to the courtroom in the convent. It seemed doubtful to me that I would be able to endure another session before the Aladdin lamp with its wild bright flame and the sinister judge with his heartless aides. But as the fresh night air hit my face, strength somehow returned to my limbs and mind.

The judge remained standing after the trial began and entered immediately upon a tirade against the United States government, the evils of our imperialistic designs on the rest of the world, particularly China and Korea. I recall that there were more than the ordinary number of soldiers crowded into the room that evening. And it seemed quite evident that the abuse shouted out by the judge against America was intended as much for the ears of the young soldiers as it was for me.

The judge seemed to spend considerable time proving that America always gets other countries to fight its wars. He illustrated his thesis by what happened during World War I and World War II in Europe and Asia. I tried to tell him that in both wars America lost a great number of men, and I was able to inject an obvious question: "Wasn't that rather what Russia did in the last war against Japan?"

It seemed incredible that so intelligent a man could make the reply he did. "That is not so," he said angrily. "Everyone knows that in the Orient it was Russia that defeated Japan, not America."

The judge seemed to be in a historical mood that Wednesday night. And I must confess he had a considerable fund of data at his command—always expounded with the usual Communist twist, of course. He explained Spain's rise to the height of world power. It was, he said, the first example of Western imperialism conquering weaker peoples. Then he spoke of France and her conquest of colonial territories and her attempt to invade China. With considerable disdain he narrated for the benefit of the Communist soldiers, standing around enthralled by the magic of his voice, the shameful conduct of Christian Britain toward China, spending several minutes on the traffic in opium, which, he said, was introduced to make helpless slaves of all Chinese.

Then he sneered: "Look at these European countries today. No one any longer considers Spain or France or England as a world power to be feared. Their prestige is gone." As he raised his arm in an arc, he compared their history to the path of the sun. They were like the sun when it was well on its way to sinking. America, he explained, was on its way also. It had already reached the high noon of its brief day; now it was on the decline also. "But," he said, "there is another sun rising over the universe, coming up strong and bright." And he raised his arm again in the start of a great arc, and said, "Soon our great China will be here at the top and will lead and rule the world."

I don't know what Stalin would say about that, but it became more and more evident among the Communist officials who questioned me and attempted to indoctrinate me that as time went on there was less and less stress to be put on the part "Big Brother Russia" was playing in China's destiny. Even the pictures of Lenin and Stalin, so much in evidence two years ago, and even one year ago, were less frequently and less prominently displayed in public places. That may be an inaccurate observation if applied to the whole of China—I know only my own area and the route I followed through South China to the coast. Still, the soft-pedaling of Russia's part in the new China makes sense to me if I know anything at all about the Chinese. No people wants to be ruled by an outside power, the Chinese people least of all.

When the judge paused in his history lecture to sip some tea, I looked around at the eager faces of the duly impressed young soldiers. I would have agreed to everything he said for a sip of that tea. But he didn't care for my opinion on things historic, nor did he seem interested in my thirst.

About this time, I was becoming hypnotized by his voice as it drifted toward me from somewhere in back of the bright light. He continued his lecture to me after his tea, and he continued to glance over my head from time to time at the soldiers. I should have liked to interrupt his abusive attack on the West and upon Christianity, but I was too weary to speak and it seemed useless to argue or to try and distinguish between the errors of Christians and the eternal truth of Christianity. It would be difficult to make myself understood and listening seemed easier to me than making the effort to speak.

The smooth-talking judge next went into a direct verbal attack on the United States. It is impossible now to recall the details of his lengthy barrage. I do remember how he sneered about the false impression still held in some parts of China that America is the land of plenty. He corrected this view by explaining to the soldiers that a handful of men in New York own all the wealth and industry. He spoke of the endless breadlines in the big cities of America, the crippled industry and the continual strikes among the dissatisfied workers. He then belittled the fighting ability of the weak American soldiers who are being sent out to conquer Korea and China. I thought to myself: if only this man could know how far the conquest of Korea and China really is from the minds of the G. I.'s fighting in the muddy rice paddies and barren hills of the wartorn Korean peninsula. If only he could know how much the young Americans in Korea yearn for their own homes and their loved ones, and how little the conquest of other lands attracts them, he would not fear or hate America.

"Don't think," he shouted, "that America is the only country that has the atom bomb." I expected him to refer to Big Brother Russia as the inventor and proud possessor of the Atom Bomb. I could hardly believe my ears when he said, "China also has the atom bomb, but few people realize that."

All this, no doubt, was to reassure the soldiers present that there was nothing to fear from American military might. He added for their comfort: "What harm could your American atom bomb do to these rice fields in this valley? Or in any other part of China? You know these high mountains here, you have climbed them. Do you think your soft American soldiers could scale them? Our soldiers can easily run up the sides of mountains, carrying a hundred pounds on their backs."

Leaning over his desk toward me he scoffed: "Furthermore, don't think we are afraid that your American government will ever attempt to come here to help you. They would never bother about you now."

I interrupted him to say: "You are correct. The American government does not even know I am here, for I am not working for the American government, but for God."

"But," he said, "you made the people think that your government would protect you, as the French and English formerly protected their nationals in China. For too many years you foreigners have been taking advantage of China, walking around our land as though it belonged to you. Those days are gone forever." And he raised his voice and glared at me angrily, repeating what he had said at least a dozen times before: "Let me see your American imperialist army come here to help you now. They would not dare! And anyhow, you are a failure as a spy and they would not trouble about you. So you might just as well confess."

The judge then changed the subject matter to the local scene. "Tell us," he said, "Is it not true that the people here are much happier now than formerly?"

I muttered, "Perhaps they are. I do not know the conditions nor the feeling of the people now, since I am removed from contact with them."

"But do you not hear much singing and see the young people dancing every day?"

"That is true," I admitted. "The young people do sing and dance very much now."

The secretary told me to come forward and write that in English. My arms were freed and I wrote the statement on the paper handed to me. I also wrote a statement to the effect that schools were in progress at all times, which literally was true. I also wrote, "There is an end of gambling," which also was quite true. I wrote, "There is no opium smoking in this area," which, so far as I could know, also was correct. When I was making my market day trips to buy rice, there never were loiterers hanging around. The Reds packed off every one who was not producing to the mines. No one stands around idle in a Communist country.

It was easy enough to admit these apparent improvements put into effect by the "new broom" even though these admissions brought no refreshment for my parched throat. Listening to the nightlong, tiresome tirades against the West was in a sense a relief from what the previous nights had brought me, although there was no relief for the twinge in my painful arms. When it was proved to me that I had ordered my Christians to refuse to pay taxes to the People's Government, I had no hesitation about signing that confession for the second time. Each time now, when I signed a confession, I was permitted to sit down. They had granted me this concession because I had told the judge it was impossible for me to write standing up. I began to look forward to the moments of relief when the ropes or tourniquets would be removed and I could sit to write my confessions.

As on the previous nights, it was the questioning about the purpose and work of the Legion of Mary that bothered me most. It disturbed me because it involved the Church and it implicated the good, fervent men and women who made up the Legion in China. It was the enraged manner of the man in black during these times that made me shudder. He would cruelly curse Our Blessed Mother and ridicule our religion because it "worshipped a woman." "How foolish," he said, "to think that this helpless woman could lead a legion that would be able to destroy the great invincible army of the People's Government." And he laughed satanically, sending a sickening feeling of disgust through my whole body. It was something more than disgust; again there was a sensation of the diabolic emanating from this man.

Never have I seen a human being so wrought up with rage as this judge when he strode toward me and demanded that I explain "this spy organization directed by you and Riberi."

He insisted that all my spy activities in Tung-an were carried on behind the front of religion and medicine. He repeated the crimes I had committed while directing the Legion of Mary: innocent Communist soldiers put to death—which again I vehemently denied, but which, he claimed, I had already confessed; helpless Chinese children poisoned in my dispensary—which witnesses maintained I had done; my attempt to deceive and oppress the poor; my work with the Legion in attempting to overthrow the benevolent People's Government. "You have signed confessions to all these crimes," he said.

When I returned to my cell that night, I felt that I hadn't adequately declared my innocence. I was more convinced than ever that it was my own blundering that had caused all the trouble for the Church here in Tung-an and for our Blessed Lady and her Legion. I was depressed as I sat there and my depression deepened when even the corporal refused to get me a drink of water.

The next morning when I awoke it was impossible for me to recall what day it was. I asked the guards several times to tell me. One of them said: "Why do you want to know? You are not going any place."

Shortly after I had my bowl of cold, left-over rice, an officer came in and advised me to be quick about confessing that I was not a priest. "You have three days to make up your mind, and if you do not acknowledge that you are a spy by that time, you will be brought before all the people of Tung-an and they —the People's Court—will see to it that you confess. They will have no mercy on you. They will gouge out your eyes before they kill you. Other priests have confessed and have been allowed to leave China. Why don't you do the same?"

He then went on to say that it would be impossible for me to continue much longer the way I was going. "The months alone in your house brought you low," he said, "and the days in this cell have taken you almost to the brink. How many more days do you think you can hold out against us?"

I shook my head and replied: "That question I cannot answer."

It was the question I had asked myself each morning, and it was becoming less certain day by day that I could last much longer. I recalled how strong had been the temptation to dive off the convent's upper balcony the night before. I knew I was struggling with the temptation not to eat any more, and so to terminate my misery that way.

Then adding up the days as best I could, I concluded that this was Holy Thursday. I was almost certain that the end of my resistance had come. I could not face the judge that night. I would give in. "Don't, dear Lord," I pleaded, "make me face that man this Holy Thursday night. The limit of my strength has been reached." I asked Our Lord to forgive me for my weakness in endurance and I tried to pray His prayers, "Thy will be done," and "Father, forgive them." I recalled His thirst and I recalled that He had endured it all innocently. But I . . . despite all my attempted prayers I could not rise from my utter despair.

It was quiet outside all day. The guards didn't seem to stare in as often as they formerly had. With my hand I wiped some pus from the sores on my face and I pressed some pus from the abscess in my ear. I sat on the boards and watched my fingers. Then, without thinking, I reached into the small watch pocket of my khaki pants. I had many times before put my hands into my pockets, empty since Lt. Leang's thorough search. This time my fingers touched something other than the cloth lining of the pocket. I pulled out a pin—a safety pin.

I gazed at it in the palm of my hands for many minutes.

Then, without deliberating on the matter at all, I opened the pin and held it between the fingers of my right hand. I put my left hand face up on my left knee. I recall it now, it was like in a dream. I thought I would just curl up on the boards unknown to the guards and let the blood flow out and it would be all over. The pin pricked lightly the flesh of my left wrist.

Then I heard my own frightened voice in English break the silence. "What are you doing? You're a priest. You can't do that."

The guards rushed to the door and windows and shouted: "What's wrong with you? Don't make so much noise in there."

I made no reply to the guards. When they had ceased looking in on my dejected form I went toward the window and in utter disgust I threw the pin out through the bars.

What I had just attempted to do upset me to the depth of my soul. I sat there on the boards trembling with mixed emotions of disgust and shame. I was angry with myself and sorry for my sin. I did not attempt then to excuse myself. It did seem at the time that it was like a hideous dream, which dissolved for me in time. Each day for many hours I had been staring at my fingers. Up until two days ago I had been providing myself in my dreams with an imaginary trial in which I would deny the absurd accusations and completely prove the falsehoods involved. The trumped-up evidence would be torn to shreds by my arguments. Where I had been failing miserably night after night before the judge, I would triumph gloriously in my imagination there in my cell. My helplessness and impotence I was transforming into unlimited forensic powers. And each time I had come out victoriously vindicated. My mind for the few hours of my dreams accepted these phantasms as representing reality.

But for the past two or three days even in my daydreams I

was continually defeated and the evidence piled against me seemed all too conclusive and overwhelming. Now for twenty-four hours a day there was a feeling of insecurity arising from my experiences with the judge and the witnesses he had assembled against me. Forgetting the number of my Christians who were remaining faithful, and the number who had already paid the supreme price of loyalty to Christ, I was disillusioned because some few had turned against me. Perhaps a psychologist would say that here, in the face of physical suffering and a consciousness of extreme worthlessness, there was to be found what technically would be called an "occasion for neurosis." Perhaps they would say that the "abnormality of the moment" would excuse my attempted violence to my own being. This much I can say, as I look back now, not for an instant did I ask the question: "Shall I do this or not?" There seemed no question of judgment or act of my will directed by my intellect. It was as if with uncontrolled senses I had found the pin and proceeded to perform the hideous act.

Many times since breathing free air and reconstructing those nightmarish events, I have asked myself how it could have happened that the medium-size safety pin had not been detected in my pocket the day Lt. Leang made his thorough search of my person. I recall that even the cuffs of my pants were examined. It hardly seems possible that it could have been placed there, or even that it had been purposely left there. I shall perhaps never know.

After the perspiration had stopped dripping onto my hands, and some calm had returned to my mind, I rebuked myself and reminded myself that unless I prayed, something equally evil might occur again. I set the matchsticks out on the boards, squatted in front of them and undertook to say the Sorrowful Mysteries of the Rosary.

Somehow my body began to feel a little stronger when I tried to use my ordeal for a purpose, when I ceased to evade my obligation to suffer for my people. I recall muttering to myself: "Oh, you of little faith . . . have confidence . . . I am with you all days, even to the end. . . ." And I reminded myself that I was one with all the Christians in the world—one Mystical Body, with Christ as its Head. Why should I fear the satanic judge who threatened me? Suppose all these men who are trying with such fiendish zeal to destroy me and the Church are one in this work with the powers of darkness, suppose all this force that at present confronts me is part of *another* "mystical body" with Satan as its head—why still should I fear, since I am one with Christ?

In answer to my prayer, Holy Thursday night I was, thank God, spared the torment of another session before the judge and the wild flame of the kerosene lamp, and for some unknown reason I did not have to go to the Sisters' Convent the following two evenings, as I had feared I would. I was not permitted to go outside even for a moment. I ate my bowl of rice and drank a small cup of warm water, and was satisfied to remain in the stench of my cell.

Early Good Friday morning one of the officials who was working with the judge's team came to the cell door and handed me about five long forms to be filled out. Hurriedly backing out of the foul air, he snapped: "False priest, we want you to write on these forms all the details of your life's history."

I muttered: "I have written my life's history for you many times."

He shouted over his shoulder: "Well, do it again, false priest, and be quick."

All over again I had to write my age, place of birth, details about my parents, schools attended, places visited. I was struggling through the final page when the official came back. He cursed me a bit for keeping him waiting while I answered the last two or three questions. When he looked at the answers I wrote, he angrily accused me of using a false handwriting. I explained: "The writing is poor because my hand shakes continually, and I find it very difficult to hold the pen firmly."

Apparently he didn't believe me—or else he saw there was no way of having me write otherwise—for he cuffed me on the side of the head and handed me a small piece of blank paper. He said: "Hurry and write your confession that you paid money to the guerrillas for the murder of Government soldiers."

I said: "I cannot write that, because it is not true."

"But," he said, "you confessed to the crime the other evening."

I said: "If I did so it was because I was not responsible for what I was signing. I cannot sign the paper you give me."

He made some remark about having the confession once in my handwriting and that he had enough to convict me, and left.

That day each time the guards came to the door they would look in and sneer and say: "False priest," or "Spy." Two Youth Corps members came to look in; they shouted: "You are no priest. Your own cook says you are not a priest." The official, when he came in with the forms, also called me a false priest. I had been telling myself all through the nervewracking hours of the nightly trials that I must never deny my priesthood. But not until Good Friday and Holy Saturday, so far as I can recall, was there ever any waivering or doubts in my mind about my priesthood no matter how often they repeated the charge.

Now as the tormenting words "false priest" kept coming through the bars of the door and the window and echoed in my ears, I began to wonder, and for the first time to doubt. It seems incredible, but I recall how I said to myself, "Maybe they have some reasons for saying I am not a priest." Then I said, "How could I have come over here to Tung-an if I were not ordained a priest at Maryknoll and sent out here?" I recalled my ordination ceremony. I was certain that it had been real. Bishop Walsh had ordained me, I remembered distinctly. But was there anything about my disposition or my intention that could have invalidated the sacrament? I tried to dismiss the absurd but tortuous doubts. I said my matchstick Rosary again.

As I squatted there moving the pieces of matches I felt a sudden sickening shock in the pit of my stomach. From the upper room in the convent, less than fifty feet away, I heard the clear, defiant voice of Sister Theresa. She was engaged in a heated discussion before the judge and his court with Ah-Hiu, my former cook. It was not possible to catch all the words that were spoken. But occasionally Ah-Hiu would raise his angry voice and the terrible reality dawned on me. I was the object of their contention. Ah-Hiu would say that I had committed some crime and Sister Theresa would deny it. The courageous voice of the loyal Sister never wavered. She answered Ah-Hiu and the judge just as she had answered the Communist indoctrinators over a year before. *Her* fine brain had not been washed nor had her loyalty been shaken. It is obvious to me now that Sister Theresa had been brought before the judge to have her testimony added to Ah-Hiu's and the Horseman's and that of all the others who had been forced to accuse me. I did not know then, on that Holy Saturday, what plans they were preparing for my Easter Sunday. It is clear to me now that, as they rehearsed the drama that was to be presented to all the people on the morrow, Sister Theresa was cast to play a leading role—if only they could break her will and make her do their bidding. I prayed for the valiant nun (for I could well understand her torment) and I thank God now that I was spared the torture of having her testify against me. Sister Theresa remained unbroken; they were afraid she might ruin their plans if she appeared at the full dress performance for which they were preparing. Only the Lord knows what it cost her that Holy Saturday morning to be loyal to her faith and to me in the face of Ah-Hiu and the satanic judge. And only the Lord knows what it has cost her since. For I have never heard her indomitable voice again.

CHAPTER SIXTEEN

Easter Sunday

As DUSK APPROACHED on Holy Saturday evening I began to get tense again, and in awful suspense I waited for the order to go to the convent courtroom. However, as on two previous nights, no "trial" was scheduled for me, and I thanked God for His merciful goodness. Perhaps the judge and his team of officials felt that they had obtained all they wanted from me for the present; or perhaps they feared that I was dangerously close to losing my mind; indeed, perhaps they wondered how it was that I had not already gone insane. As I look back now there seems no doubt that they had brought me very close to the border line.

While it was a refreshing relief to be spared the ordeal of the "private trials" for those three days, still my mind was not free from torments. I thought constantly of the Blessed Sacrament hidden in the rectory, and I wondered if anyone had made a search of the rooms and discovered It. Maybe some officers had already moved into my quarters to live. I was nauseated by the stench of the foul cell; my dysentery was returning; my parched throat made me constantly yearn for water.

For a few minutes I would squat and say a decade of the Rosary as I moved the pieces of matches from the right to the left; but most of the time I just sat and stared at my fingers or gazed out the small window high on the wall. From time to time I would talk out loud about my priesthood, going over the ordination ceremony, recalling my assignment to the Kweilin mission and my appointment by Monsignor Romaniello to the pastorate at Tung-an. And I said to myself that though it might be possible to admit to all the crimes of which I was accused, I must never sign any statement that I was not a priest. As I lay down to sleep, I thought of the glorious feast of Easter that was to come with the dawn—victory, hope, resurrection. Maybe it would mean victory and hope for me too.

Easter morning dawned damp and bleak. My spirit was one with the weather. About an hour after dawn a guard opened the cell door and hurriedly passed a bowl of rice to me. He said: "Hurry with your rice, there is not much time. Take care of the needs of nature. Something big is going to happen today and you have to be ready in a few minutes."

Forgetting all about the dreadful public trial with which I had been threatened, I naively asked. "What is going to happen?"

A sergeant came to the door at that moment and he answered my question: "Today is market day," he said, "and we have something specially arranged for you. Now look," he added, "you are going to be in a position for several hours where you cannot move. Don't drink any water."

That sounded like a needless piece of advice, because there was no water for me to drink anyhow.

The sergeant barked out a command and the squad of

soldiers that had been assigned to watch me during these past two weeks formed a double line outside the door. They were carrying rifles with drawn bayonets. I still was not fully aware of what was going on. Everything seemed blurred, my legs were weak and stiff, and my mouth was parched. The sergeant ordered me outside, and I took my place between the two grim lines of soldiers. He gave the command to march and I staggered along, out through the mission gate down the dirt bus road toward the market place. The street was jammed with people, even this early. The crowd seemed larger and more excited than on any previous market day that I could recall. They stood to one side and made a passageway for us to pass.

I muttered to the guard: "Where are we going?" He barked: "You just march. Keep your eyes down, and don't talk."

We marched off the bus road down the main alleyway of shops. People were pushing and milling about like cattle herded into a stockyard. The soldiers angrily shouted at the mob to make way. I stared at the ocean of faces as through a mist. At the end of this crowded mart there was a huge newly-constructed bamboo shed. It was a wide hangar-type affair, open at one end and with a large stage about five feet off the ground at the farther end. Already most of the seats were filled with people. We walked down the middle of the shed, up the side stairs, through the wings, and onto the platform.

The stage had an almost festive touch about it. Brown cotton draperies covered the rear and sides; a large picture of Mao Tse-tung filled the center of the drapes, flanked by pictures of other Chinese Communist officials. So far as I can recall there was no picture of Stalin or Lenin in evidence. There were three tables arranged somewhat in the rear and to the center of the stage, and behind the tables sat the same team of officials who had been conducting my "private trials" for so many nights. In the middle of the group was the man who said he had been sent to Tung-an to judge me. Near the tables a Communist woman official dressed in a blue uniform sat with pencil and notebook. The sergeant and the guards who escorted me to the platform took their places off to the side. Two guards remained near me, one on my left and the other on my right.

From my knowledge of the procedure followed in the numerous accusation meetings and trials held in the field near the mission, I suspected that along with me this Easter morning market day, there would be several other criminals presented to the people for judgment. There seemed no doubt in my mind that this would be my final trial and my final hour—the end of the long ordeal.

I had no idea that the whole spectacle had been arranged to deal with me alone. As I turned to face the smiling judge and his staff of officials, I looked up at the hideous caricatures some clever hand had drawn of me. In large Chinese characters my name was printed under each cartoon. In one, I recall, I was dressed as a priest in cassock. I was holding aloft a crucifix—under my picture were the words "false priest". In another I was a revolting devil, complete with horns and tail. But the cartoon that filled me most with loathing was the large drawing of the Legion of Mary standard. In this picture I was sitting at a table with a vicious looking Uncle Sam slyly whispering in my ear. On the side were words explaining the espionage activity of the Legion.

At a signal from the judge the guards turned me around and nudged me to the front of the platform, just to the right of the center of the stage. The mob of at least six thousand people was a sea of heads, expressionless but expectant. As the faces came into focus I sickened to see that almost all the people in the front part of the big shed were Christians. There were hundreds of them sitting there with downcast eyes, not only my own Tung-an Christians, but also Christians from other parishes of the diocese as well. Could these evil men have told the helpless Christians they were free to come to the Tung-an mission for Easter? Did these God-denying men *know* it was Easter? I never was able to discover whether or not the Christians had been promised a religious ceremony by their pastor that day. Only one thing seems certain: the diabolical design to seat the Christians in vantage spots in the front of the crowd to see their pastor humiliated and accused and condemned.

For a fleeting moment, as I looked out on these Christians, my mind went back to other Easters here in Tung-an. I could see these same men and women coming through the mission gate as they did in former years with joy and laughter on the lips and peace in their hearts. On Easter they seemed always to exude the triumphant spirit of the Resurrection. But during the past two years all that had been changed. Except for the youth standing around on the sides and in the rear, there was no feeling of triumph. The Christians in the front rows did not lift their eyes to mine, and that, in a sense, consoled me. My heart bled for them, herded here in terror, against their wills.

The young Communist woman official in the blue uniform stepped to the front of the stage and in a clear voice requested that everyone be "quiet throughout the very important trial of this American imperialist spy." Children and babies who made any noise were to be removed from the audience. As a reminder that the whole program was being carried out in the spirit of "true democracy" she added, "Does everyone agree that this is a good idea?" In real democratic Communist fashion everyone unanimously agreed that it was.

When she finished her introductory remarks one of the officials working with the judge came over to me, and angrily told me that I was not to move or talk at any time. I was to keep my eyes down and my head bowed always. My hands were not to be tied or placed in tourniquets; they were to remain straight down by my sides. Then he explained to the two guards standing beside me that they were responsible for any deviation from these instructions. It was clear that this trial was to be very different from the farces conducted in the convent upper room.

Then the drama for which these thousands of people were gathered got under way.

The first "witness" called upon to testify against me was the fifteen-year-old girl. Apparently unafraid of the huge crowd, and with a great deal of emotion and a surprising amount of eloquence, she went through the charges she had brought against me in the previous trials. She went into considerable detail about my forming the Legion of Mary for spy work; she told how I had poisoned her brother with drugs; she even added another murder or two for good measure. By this time she had worked herself to the front of the stage directly in front of me, and from time to time she would turn toward me gesticulating angrily.

When the girl finished, her face flushed red with the excitement of the moment, a young officer took a large megaphone and slowly bellowed out a recapitulation of her absurd accusations. Then he asked in a loud voice: "What now is the judgment of the People's Court regarding this criminal?"

Rising like a crowd at a football game they shouted: "Kill him—give him the penalty of death!"

When the mob quieted down the next witness came from the left wing of the stage. The voice I heard was strange to me, and forgetting the instructions not to move, I lifted my head with instinctive curiosity to see who the man was. One of the guards remembered his instructions and poked me with his gun, and cursing me he hissed: "Eyes down!"

The witness I glanced at was dressed in a Communist army uniform, and he announced to the judge and to the people that he had been requested to represent the Christians of the county seat of Ping-lo. After I heard him speak for a few minutes it seemed almost certain that he was not even a Christian. He read solemnly a declaration stating that the Christians of Ping-lo had discovered that "the spy, Chin Peh-teh," was not a priest, but an agent of the imperialist American government. He further stated that the Christians of Ping-lo and all the neighboring villages repudiated me and were ashamed of the crimes I had committed against the People's Government of China.

This testimony was followed by similar statements read by "representatives" from at least fifteen neighboring parishes. And after each witness finished the young officer shouted his résumé through the megaphone.

Without lifting my eyes I knew the possessors of the next voices coming from the wings. I recognized at once Chin Y-chai, the guerrilla organizer, the ex-guerrilla quartermaster, and my ex-friend, the Horseman.

Chin Y-chai I was sure most of the mob knew, at least by name. He eloquently explained to the people his recent change of heart. Whatever he had said or done against the People's Government was done through ignorance. He had been misled into activities which he now humbly acknowledged were sins against the Chinese people and its new government. "I throw myself now," he said dramatically, "on the mercy of the

People's Court and on the mercy of our great savior, Mao Tse-tung."

Then Chin Y-chai moved closer to me and with uncontrollable anger he pointed his finger at me and shouted: "But this man, this spy agent of the American imperialists, is the one who misled me. He is the one who organized and directed our wicked action against the People's Army. And now he stands here and refuses to admit his guilt and to confess his crimes."

In a clear, loud voice Chin told in great detail how I had met with them, planned their "shameful deeds," and ordered them never to surrender, but to fight to the end.

Solemnly and humbly the guerrilla leader ended with the usual oath: "If what I have spoken is not the truth, I beg the People's Court to behead me."

Then he backed away from the center of the stage near me and the quartermaster stepped forward.

These voices were familiar to me now; I had heard them so many times during those soul-wracking sessions in the Sisters' convent room. And I had heard the words before and the accusations before, but never had I heard them announced with such conviction before. As the quartermaster thundered out his testimony I was wondering if the thousands of people out in front of me were being deceived. The ring of certitude in the accusers' voices, their natural penchant for acting, made me again wonder who was right—and again doubts began to haunt me. These meetings that they spoke of—they mentioned the year and the month and the day on which these events took place, even the hour of the day. They mentioned places where we had met and I knew these places, I had been to them, homes of Christians, or shops along the market place. I had stopped many times at the Horseman's home to ask him to take packages to a neighbor priest. It was the Horseman himself who testified that I visited his home often to conduct meetings. He told the mob how uneasy he was when I called, how unwilling he was to have me in his home, but there was nothing he could do about it because I had a secret control over his mind.

As on so many occasions during the private trials, if I myself found reasons to doubt my own opinion, how could the minds of most of these people fail to be convinced when they listened to testimony so convincingly presented?

The sun hid his face during the long hours of the morning session, but the heat began to burn through the mist and clouds about noon. My legs were becoming numb; I wanted desperately to stretch my limbs and my neck, but each attempt I made to move was met by a jab from a guard's bayonet. Several times I started to wipe the trickling perspiration from my face, but my hands were not permitted to alter their dangling apelike posture.

After these three prize witnesses had finished their testimony and had backed off the stage, the summary of their statements was given to the people through the megaphone. And again the mob, obviously more incensed than ever against me, clamored for my death.

Without any apparent signal from the master of arms, a woman next hysterically rushed onto the stage carrying a small child in her arms. She put the child on the platform near me and reached toward me to slap my face, madly shouting at the same time that I had blinded her child. She turned to the crowd and repeated the charge. The short, fat man with the camera, who had reappeared, was on the alert and shot a picture of the screaming child as well as one of its screaming mother.

A man came forward next to accuse me of ordering the people not to pay the just taxes to the People's Government.

Another man rushed toward me shouting that I had directed him and others to enlist with the guerrillas and to fight against the army of the People's Government. I did not see either of their faces nor did I recognize either of their voices.

Needles were shooting through my legs, and the back of my hunched shoulders felt as though I had a bag of sand on them. I kept murmuring short prayers to Our Blessed Lord to help and direct me. I tried to remind myself of His unjust trial and His divine innocence. I was wondering what I would say when it came my time to address the people in my own defense. Would I be able to talk with my tongue swollen and parched? Would I take each of the accusations separately, or defiantly shout out that the whole affair was an absurd and mocking lie? Would they believe me after this overwhelming accumulation of plausible evidence so devastatingly heaped up against me?

I raised my eyes, my head still bent, to the Christians in the front row, but none of them would meet my gaze. After one of the testimonies, when the mob arose, I saw one or two Christians hesitate to rise. Once when all the mob raised their clenched fists in the air my eyes met those of one of my Catholics. He embarrassingly altered his gesture to adjusting his hat. At least that was some consolation, and it made it somewhat easier to be patient and silent. Maybe others, maybe many others, felt the same way.

How long I had been standing I could not know; certainly it must have been more than four hours. It seemed that soon there would be an end to the drama, which had been well rehearsed for so many weary nights in the convent. But I reminded myself that there must be more—I could not hope that Ah-Hiu, my cook, would fail to appear. He, I knew, was the most damaging of all the witnesses against me. He had been my loyal helper; he had lived closer to me than anyone else; he knew everything about me; his testimony would be listened to with eagerness and acceptance.

And now from the corner of my eye I could see him strutting from the wings. He addressed the judge, the officials and the people. Always Ah-Hiu had been an entertaining performer, and for a poorly educated man a most convincing and eloquent speaker. But never had he had an audience as large and attentive watching him and listening to him. He had charmed crowds before, he would really sway one today. Ah-Hiu, overcome with bitterness and fury against me, did not let his manager, the judge, or his audience down that day.

The change in him that I had noticed on Palm Sunday when he appeared against me in the private trial was more pronounced on Easter. Even before he began his speech his face was flushed red with anger. He pointed at me and shouted: "This man here, by means of the narcotics he gave me, has for many years fooled me into obeying his wicked commands. Cleverly he has tricked me into believing that he was a genuine Spiritual Father. But now I understand clearly that he has all this time been offending against all the commandments of God while spying on the Chinese people. And now I will show the People's Court in what manner I discovered that he was a false priest by examining his conscience—as he so often told us to do ourselves."

Then he started down the decalogue as he had done on Palm Sunday and at several of the evening sessions. Cursing me, he walked toward me and struck my face. He told the people how I never prayed; how I cursed the Chinese people; how I worked on Sunday; how I refused to return to my dying mother when she called for me. "This he did," Ah-Hiu added, "not because of his love for the Chinese Christians, but because of his love for the imperialist Americans for whom he is working."

Jabbing his finger repeatedly into my cheeks he went on for some time on the fifth commandment. There was little change in his testimony from what he had already given in the convent. With added vehemence he told his Easter Sunday audience how I had deliberately given poison to people in the dispensary, had even taught him how to administer poison. Ah-Hiu went into considerable detail about my activities with the guerrilla soldiers.

Chin Y-chai, standing off to the side, substantiated the charge, shouting: "The People's witness speaks the truth. I have been a witness to what he has testified."

The Horseman, missing his cue for the moment, stepped forward to say that against his will he had taken messages from me to the bandit guerrillas.

The quartermaster then said that he had accepted the messages delivered to him by the Horseman.

After each corroborating interruption, Ah-Hiu, frothing with anger, chafing with impatience, would take over again, poking his finger in my face for emphasis. As during the private trials he had very little to say about the sixth commandment. However, he did add, without any attempt at details, that he had much evidence that my relations with Sister Theresa were improper. It was the only part of Ah-Hiu's testimony that he did not deliver with conviction.

On surer grounds, he told the audience how I had cheated the people, had refused to pay for the food purchased on the market, and how I had taught him to steal and cheat. He showed that I had lied many times about the People's Government. Among other things, he said: "This man claimed that

my back on God or denying my religious belief. I want it understood that I am still a Catholic."

Though he hated me I uttered a quiet blessing upon him. It warmed my heart to hear at such a time and in such a place his act of Faith; and I was sure that many a Catholic sitting unwillingly in front of me took courage from his words.

CHAPTER SEVENTEEN

Unanimous Decision

WHY THE MAD MOB, worked into a frenzy of hate toward me by the vicious lies of the witnesses, did not rush the stage and drag my numb body off to a violent death will always remain a great mystery to me. The particularly vehement verbal attack on me by the ex-guerrilla leader Chin Y-chai and the venomous destruction of my whole character by Ah-Hiu had certainly moved the crowd to a high pitch of fury. Each time the young officer shouted his resumé through the megaphone and asked, "What shall we do with this infamous American spy?" the mob seemed more and more violent as they rose with clenched fists and shouted for my death.

By this time, it didn't much matter to me what happened. Death—quick, merciful death—would be my deliverer. I was numb now through my whole body; my hands and arms dangled limp and lifeless by my knees; my shoulders drooped forward, and my jaw hung open on my chest. It did not seem possible that they could drag on the travesty any longer. Yet the cruel mob remained unsatiated. Most of them seemed to enjoy the spectacle of their helpless victim enmeshed inescapably in the web of the carefully constructed plot.

I was past thinking; I was nodding limply to the convincing accumulation of evidence. Only one thing I kept repeating to myself: "You are a priest, you are a priest. Remember that."

It was the hopelessness of the situation that was hardest to take—my aloneness, the fact that there was no one to say one word in my defense. Past acts performed in charity were brought forth now to prove my treacherous guilt.

Shortly after the Reds took over Tung-an, a poor peasant came to tell me that his son had been captured by the guerrillas and they had threatened to kill him unless a guarantee could be procured testifying that the young man was not a Communist. The old man begged me to write a note saying that his son was a Catholic and not a Red. I knew this old man and his family well and I felt certain that the young man had no Communistic leanings. So I wrote the note testifying that the young man was, so far as I knew, not a Communist. He was released and I recall the tears of gratitude shed by both father and son when they came to thank me.

There had been no mention of this incident in any of the private trials. It had been saved for this Easter Sunday drama, presented to the People's Court to prove my influence and authority over the guerrillas.

The risk I took in pleading for his son's life had been forgotten. There was no gratitude now in the old man's voice. A blow in the face would have been easier to take. But then, I knew that this poor simple man, if free to express his real feeling, would never have acted the way he did. Still, how few there must have been in that vast mob who realized my innocence. For many, no doubt, had heard how this man's son had been saved through my intercession. Even I began to see the rashness of my act and how it could now be construed as criminal. Again I wondered. And again as the old man continued his feigned attack on me, I prayed that I might faint, though still somehow I retained consciousness. My head was so light I thought at times I would simply topple off the stage into the laps of the Christians in the front seats.

It was after the officer with the megaphone had shouted his résumé of this accusation and had asked for the judgment of the People's Court that my eyes met those of a Christian in the front row. This man was just in the process of raising his hand in the gesture meaning "Execute him", when he looked directly at me. Instead of shooting his hand in the air, he raised it to his head and ran it over his hair. Then, realizing what he had done, he nervously glanced to each side and up onto the stage to see if he had been detected. It was the one humorous incident of that entire tragic Easter Sunday. And for me it was like a refreshing drink to relieve the bitterness of the day.

On another occasion during one of the cook's accusations when he was continually slapping my face, I looked out over the sea of faces and saw two Christian women near the front in tears, and an unknown woman near them also crying. I thanked God for their genuine expression of sympathy. And I blessed them silently.

The morning began to seem weeks ago. There seemed no end of the day. No longer was I trembling, my whole body was lifeless. I stood with the indifference of a corpse at my own autopsy.

My heart sunk still lower when Ah-Hiu, the star witness, again strutted to the front of the stage beside me. Could there possibly be anything that he had omitted? What more could these evil men inject into his changed and well-washed brain. It was almost an anticlimax—yet he seemed more worked up than when he had "examined by conscience" on the ten commandments earlier in the day.

Ah-Hiu told the people that he had one more accusation to make and then he would rest his case with the People's Court for judgment. The mob was to be the jury and the judge—on the Communist presumption that an incited mad mob can be just.

My former cook, his anger still at white heat, told how I had poisoned great numbers of Communist soldiers. In giving them powdered milk to drink, I had deliberately used unboiled water. As a result the soldiers contracted typhoid and many died. He repeated the charge that I had taught him several ways to administer poison under the guise of medicine.

However, at long last, the cook said that his testimony against me was ended. He spoke for about ten more minutes explaining to the people that if he had appeared in the past to be loyal to me, and to have assisted me in my espionage activities, it was only because of the drugs I fed him which made him a slave to my will. "I had no will of my own and that is how he fooled me into doing his bidding. But now I confess to the People's Court and beg mercy for my past association with this American spy devil. I leave the judgment to be passed against this great enemy of the People's Government of China to the People's Court."

The last words I heard from the lying lips of the once trustworthy Ah-Hiu were these: "If what I have spoken is not the truth, I beg the People's Court to behead me."

Would I now be called upon for a statement in my own defense? Would the judge request me to reply to the accusations brought against me? I decided that I would make no attempt to answer the witnesses. I would shout out only: "It is a sham trial. I have been framed. All the words you've heard are lies—lies." But would they believe me? Was not the evidence, so convincingly presented, overwhelming against me? Could my voice any longer utter sound? My jaw would no longer move when I tried to close my mouth.

However, it was not necessary for me to try to decide what I should say, or see if I could voice my thoughts in words. The inhuman judge in black, silent during these long hours, was introduced to the mob. Angrily he strutted to the front of the stage near me. For the first time, his name was mentioned in my presence. The official who introduced him said, "I now present to the people Judge Tien."

His long recapitulation of the entire proceedings must have wearied the crowd almost as much as it wearied me. He went back several years to statements I had made at that time. He quoted confessions signed by me. He told the people the history of my entire life, which the famous secret intelligence of the People's Government had been able to discover about me. The schools I attended, the places in China where I had formerly been stationed and the cities I had visited. Intimate details of my family, my brother's employment, and how my brother would disown me for working for the Wall Street capitalists, because he was a worker like the people against whom I had plotted. Actually, my brother is a contractor and engineer, but in giving them the information I had used the word in Chinese for builder.

Judge Tien told the silent mob that their secret police had discovered that I was an officer in the American Army (Colonel, he said). They knew my salary. He told them how they had watched my spy activity after I had formed the reactionary Legion of Mary acting as the chief agent for my espionage work. Then it was that the People's Government had learned and proved that I was not a priest at all, but used religion and medicine as my fronts to deceive the people and destroy the People's Government.

Why does he go on, I thought. Why doesn't he put an end to the day and order me to be taken to the field and shot?

But he did not stop. He spent considerably more time talking about the Legion of Mary and its evil influence in China.

More bitterly than I had previously heard him speak, he said: "You have seen in the newspapers how this spy ring of the Legion of Mary operates among you and in other parts of China." He told the angered mob about my association with Archbishop Riberi and Father McGrath, and that I was, as everyone knew, the dreaded leader of this espionage group in Southwest China. So many times during his frenzied address to the mob the judge would point disdainfully and angrily at me, almost putting his quivering finger into my eyes: "*Chin Peh-teh, ni pu shih shen fu*—Greene, you are no priest—you are no priest!" How many times he said those words. They are still ringing in my spinning head. "You are no priest." I would try to whisper to myself weakly, "Remember, whatever else happens, don't deny your priesthood—you *are* a priest. You *are* a priest, remember."

I tried feebly and hopelessly to pray. I was without feeling in all my members. It made not the slightest stir within me when the judge paused from time to time and shouted at the aroused mob: "What shall we do to a devilish spy such as this Chin Peh-teh?" Nor did I respond in any way when their angry "Execute him! Execute him!" filled the air.

He spoke about the mercy of Mao who would forgive even this most treacherous of spies, if only he would confess and ask for pardon. Only at that moment, so far as I can now recall, did I feel an anxious movement in my breast. Would he now try to force me, before this frenzied mob, to confess that I was not a priest, and that the Legion of Mary was a spy organization?

But the judge did not apparently think that my confession was necessary. He would now announce the sentence, he said. "The People's Court has heard the evidence of truthful witnesses against this lying spy; the judgment of the people is fair and just and unanimous. It is your judgment that this American devil has been guilty of espionage against our government, and it is the will of the people that he be beheaded."

I expected a great cheer to go up from the mob; instead there was an awful silence. The sentence the judge passed on me I heard, but the words made no impression on my mind. It was the judge's "*Wan liao*—it is finished," that brought me back to reality. I breathed a grateful sigh when I heard his heavy shoes walk off the stage. I was thankful that at last it was ended, and I was relieved to know that there would be no request for me to make a statement or a confession.

As the mob started to rise and restlessly stretch their limbs, the young woman in blue who had started the proceedings six or seven hours before, came to the front of the stage and announced the end of the Court and ordered everyone to return to his home.

A guard pushed me and ordered me to get moving, but it was impossible for me to move my feet. I had no control over my muscles. It was as though I had been put in a barrel of fresh cement and left for a day while the mortar hardened. Finally, with a few more inhuman shoves by the guards, mobility returned; and I shuffled off the stage mumbling unintelligibly to myself. Again the guards barked out their orders for the people to make way for us to move through. I didn't see anyone; I walked as in a stupor, through a heavy mist. As we passed the execution field next to the mission property, one of the guards said to me: "You're lucky you are not lying out there right now."

I couldn't comment—I just mumbled, I could not move my mouth; my jaw was still hanging grotesquely off toward my shoulder. Another guard said: "Did you hear the sentence of the People's Court?" I mumbled something. "You are to be beheaded, do you know that?" Again I grunted some unintelligible sound. "Remember, Mao the Savior is very merciful. You should beg for forgiveness."

They opened the door of my cell and pushed me inside; I remember falling lifeless on the boards and I recall that the sun was going down over the bamboo trees as I looked out the top of the window. I did not want to think of the number of hours I had stood numb and disgraced before that mob, but I later estimated it must have been at least seven. I lost consciousness—there was a gap. Then I recall awakening and feeling the blood coming back into my legs and I found my jaw would move a little. I knelt down for a minute, but said no prayer so far as I can recall.

The guards were watching me, and after a bit the corporal opened the door and softly asked me if I'd like some water to drink. I couldn't think of the word for yes, nor could I utter it if I had. I nodded, and he understood. When he handed the refreshing drink to me, I nodded again and when I looked in his eyes to express my feeling of gratitude, I was sure there was a sign of sympathy there for me as he took back the empty bowl.

That night was the worst night of my life. There was an almost tangible, tar-like sticky blackness around me. I could feel it on all sides of me. I couldn't explain it then, nor can I now. But I could almost see this encompassing black mass above my head and around me. I was in it, unable to escape it.

I remember how I tried again to say the *Memorare* and the Hail Mary. I was trying to dismiss from my tortured mind the thought that there was the ordeal of a forced confession still to come. If only they would come in and take me to the field now and shoot me, even behead me if that was the sentence passed. I had watched so many die so quickly there in the field. It would be so easy. Bang! and it would be all over. I wondered if I would hear only the command of the sergeant. It wouldn't matter.

The sleepless hours that followed were a torturous preparation for what I thought was an inevitable end. I prayed that somehow a priest might come to me—maybe Father Ma, the Chinese priest, was in the neighborhood and would come to me. So many months had passed without the opportunity to confess. I had heard that many priests are called that way, with no opportunity to receive the Last Sacraments. Then I said: "I must make a good act of contrition now, because when the moment comes in which I am to die, I may be too exhausted to do it properly."

There were times when I was tempted to call the guards and ask them to tell the judge that I was prepared to confess everything that they accused me of—if he would allow me first just one moment alone in my quarters. There seemed no possible chance now to take care of the Blessed Sacrament.

I knew there were meetings going on over in the Sisters' convent; I could see the reflection from the big flame of the Aladdin kerosene lamp. I wondered what they were preparing for me. What would the morrow bring? If only I could stop for a moment in my room in the rectory before they took me out for execution, I wouldn't mind then how they put me to death.

As I look back now, it was, I am sure, the mental torture that came from my thoughts of the possible desecration of the Blessed Sacrament that kept my mind off my personal physical pains. I told myself that I must not die until I took care of that one obligation.

I lay down and in the distance I could hear the drums of Ten Tan Ko beating, and I knew that the young people there were dancing. The rhythmic rumble went on, but I was not certain whether the drums were beating in the Tung-an hills or only in my mind. The drums were the drums of death—the dance was the dance of death. In my weary mind, I could see the youth dancing. It was the dance that preceded the trials on the stage. They were beating now for me, for my death.

I must have dropped again into unconsciousness. When I came to this time, I was on my knees. The cell was filled with a sea of faces and I could hear the mob clamoring for my death. With great effort I stiffly got up and walked to the window for a breath of pure air. As I looked out, my eyes were drawn away from the stars to the large wild flame of the Aladdin lamp, still burning brightly on the upper balcony of the Sisters' convent. A group of men were sitting around in heated discussion. I could hear nothing clearly except occasionally, "American Devil," or "The Legion of Mary." Naturally, I felt that more horrible torture was being planned for me—though I could not imagine what further torments, short of death, they could devise.

As I looked back toward the stars in the black sky, I somehow recalled that it was Easter Sunday morning in America. Many gay, happy people had already been to Church; children in their new Easter clothes were enjoying the triumphant thrill of our Savior's victory. I knew there were friends of mine and friends of Maryknoll's and friends of the missions who were praying for me—praying that I might be strong and that, if it be God's will, I might survive. There was no way for them to know what had happened to me. It was possible that one day my superiors might learn of my death and where my body lay.

Looking out into the blackness that had enveloped Tung-an, I wondered if another priest one day soon might have the opportunity to bring my Christians together for prayer and instruction. Would he, if I were not around, be able to tell them that all they had heard that Easter day was lies? If I should escape this death that now ensnared me in its grasp, would I one day see my people come back to me one by one, whispering "Spiritual Father, I knew that you were innocent; forgive me for joining in the viciously false spectacle that humiliated you?" Please God one day I may have the opportunity to forgive every one of them.

CHAPTER EIGHTEEN

Their Purpose Achieved

I RECALL NOTHING further of Easter night. My exhausted body and frayed nerves could stand no more. I dropped into unconsciousness again while the muffled voices on the Sisters' balcony mumbled on.

The surly guards awakened me Easter Monday morning, and, with an air more of disgust than anger, shouted at me to get ready and come with them.

"Where are we going?" I asked dreamily.

"Never mind where, just come," they impatiently answered.

They took me again to the large upper room in the convent. The judge with his sinister smile was behind the table. As I approached the middle of the room, he snarled at me: "I sentenced you yesterday to be beheaded. Do you know that?"

I muttered dejectedly: "Yes, yes, I know."

But he could not understand my mumbled response, and he snapped, "Repeat what I just said to you."

I had understood his words, but it was impossible for me to give them expression.

The judge repeated them himself for me, bringing the side of his hand across his neck as he said: "I sentenced you to be beheaded, do you understand that?"

I tried again to say that what he said was understood, but the only sound I could emit was a mumbled "Uh."

Thinking that I could not follow their conversation, one of the officials whispered: "The guards were right, his mind is gone."

The judge gave him a knowing nod and threw a glance of disgust in my direction. Then, I recall, he launched forth into a long recital about the mercy of Mao Tse-tung. When he finished, one of the other officials came toward me and asked if I had understood the judge's merciful words. I murmured something in answer. Then the official slowly said: "The kind judge has commuted your sentence. Do you understand? You are to be deported from China forever. Are you not grateful to the judge?" He said I was to be "rolled out" of China. The term is a slang expression meaning thrown out head over heels. And he repeated it, for he was not sure that I had understood his meaning.

I understood all too well, but my heart was far from elated. I did not want to think that the end of my work for the people of Tung-an had come, nor did I like to think that my Christians would be without a pastor. But most of all, I thought of the Blessed Sacrament hidden in the small room in the rectory. Furthermore, I had learned by this time that it was impossible to believe any words from their lying tongues. I was sure they would take me from Tung-an to the county seat and repeat the ordeal there before a still larger crowd.

Then the judge spoke out again: "Don't think that we are letting you off free. We have had our benefit from you—our purpose has been achieved. You are not the important spy you think you are. We are after the big spy leaders operating in China. You go back to America now—and shamefully face your brother, who is one with the laboring class. You are now forty years of age, but remember, you will never see fifty. Do you know why? Because in ten years we shall have America. The Communists in America will take care of you." And again he made the sinister gesture of lopping off one's head. "Go back to your country and tell the people of America how kind and merciful Mao has been to you. Tell them of the vigor of the new fearless China."

He was about to dismiss me when he added: "You may take with you any of your clothes you are able to carry."

Excitedly I spoke for the first time with some semblance of intelligible sound: "May I return to my quarters to get my clothes for the journey?"

He snapped: "No, tell the guards what you need and they will get them for you."

I don't know what prompted me to speak the words that then came to my lips. Without deliberation, without even knowing what I was saying, I stammered to the pagan judge, "There are three things I need very badly."

He barked: "What are they?"

I answered distractedly: "I need a pyx, a cassock, and a stole."

The judge, not certain that he had understood correctly, looked inquisitively at the other officials. But they could give him no help; they merely shook their heads. Obviously, not one of them knew the nature of the objects for which I asked. The judge gave an evasive answer, saying, "We shall see about them later on." Then he impatiently dismissed me.

My heart was sick again as the guards led me back and shoved me into the depressing stench of my cell. Perhaps they think, I said to myself, that I have wired the rectory with traps to blow up the place once I am inside again. Still, there was one feeble flicker of hope left that the guards might permit me to return for a minute now that the heartless judge had dismissed me. But when I begged them to allow me to go to my rectory for a brief visit to procure my things, they growled angrily that I should not bother them with business that had already been decided by the judge.

Most of Easter Monday is still a blank in my memory. I vaguely recall faces coming to the bars of the window to look in on me and utter some curses at me. Still, most of the day was a long senseless gap during which I just sat and stared at my fingers, wondering what would be the next step in their diabolical plot to exterminate me. However, no one, so far as I can recall, entered the cell all that day, and I fell asleep shortly after dusk.

Very early the next morning the police sergeant came to the cell and shouted: "Come with me."

Outside the door were waiting the corporal who had several times showed some kindness toward me, and the same squad of ten soldiers with drawn bayonets. I fell in between the soldiers, having no idea where they were going to take me. The warm sunshine of that April morning felt good and seemed somewhat to revive me. As we started along the walk from the mission chapel prison toward the main gate, I noticed a charcoal-burning bus outside with its motor running. I thought for certain they were escorting me directly to the bus.

My heart did a somersault when the sergeant abruptly barked, "Squads right march," and we turned toward the rectory. There was such a pounding of my heart within me as we climbed the stairs to my room that there was intense pain behind my ears.

It was apparent that no one had been using the rectory during the two weeks since I had been taken to the chapel prison. And I thought, "The Blessed Sacrament—I'm sure they have not touched It."

Once upstairs I started immediately and instinctively for the small room. The sergeant jerked me around and said, "That is not your room, go in here." And he shoved me into my bedroom. I pointed to some clothes that I wanted for the trip. They took a few things from the closet, and I started again toward the small unsealed room next to mine. Again the sergeant grabbed me by the arm and told me not to move and not to touch anything. "Point," he repeated, "point to whatever you want, but remember, you can take nothing made of metal. And hurry, we haven't much time."

I said: "There is nothing more I want here. I want some things from the next room."

The sergeant said, " But *this* is your room, isn't it? Don't forget, once we leave this room we are not coming back. Now let's look quickly at what you want in this next room." And he repeated: "Don't touch anything in there."

At this moment my heart was like a piston banging in my breast. By chance I was standing next to the corporal as we crowded into the small room. One of the soldiers pointed to the large beautifully carved crucifix hanging on the wall to the left; he started toward it and the others followed him. As it would to young untutored pagans the world over, the strange sight of the Man hanging on a cross aroused their curiosity. Their minds were distracted for a moment from me and from the purpose of their mission. They gathered around the crucifix, discussing the naked Corpus nailed to the cross. The sergeant elbowed his way to the front of the group and began to explain how Christians "worship this thing."

The corporal was not distracted. He stuck to me like a burr. I whispered to him excitedly: "Quick, over there—get that box for me, please."

Just inside the door to the right was the small bookcase in the corner of which was the metal cashbox covered with a large towel.

"What is it?" he asked curiously.

"Never mind, get it. Open it quick and I'll show you what it is."

His curiosity overcame his fear that it might be a trap to blow the place up and he reached over and took out the cashbox and put it on a dresser beside the bookcase. My heart was pounding in my ears.

"What is it?" he asked again.

"*Pu yao pa*—Don't be afraid," I said, bursting with pent-up excitement. "Open it quickly".

While the soldiers were still listening to the sergeant's explanation of the crucifix, the corporal, sensing the earnestness of my appeal, unwrapped the towel and opened the cover of the cashbox. I looked inside and saw that the pyx containing the Blessed Sacrament wrapped in a linen cloth was still there. A thrill went through my whole body.

I started to reach for it. The corporal struck me. "What *is* it?" he asked, mystified.

"Look," I whispered, "when we Christians pray we go like this. . . . " Quicker by far than it takes to tell it, I removed the lid from the pyx and took the Blessed Sacrament in my trembling fingers and conveyed It to my tongue.

The corporal shouted: "Stop—don't swallow that!" Then to the others: "Quick, he's eaten something." The sergeant, like the corporal, thinking no doubt that I had either taken poison or destroyed some secret spy code, furiously grabbed me and shook me—demanding that I spit out what I had taken in my mouth. He angrily cursed me and yelled: "We told you not to touch anything, didn't we? Why did you touch that thing and eat it?" And he struck me in the face.

But even though my parched and swollen tongue had for a tantalizing moment refused to swallow the precious Host, I finally was able to consume It. Nothing mattered now; a profound calm came over me, a great joy bubbled up in me like a great refreshing spring. I was ready to suffer any punishment the soldiers, or the judge, or anyone else might inflict upon me. I explained to the sergeant: "It's all right now. I was merely showing the corporal what we do when we pray."

The sergeant angrily threw the few things I had selected into a bag—and strangely enough he allowed me to take the small pyx with me, even though it was made of metal. I changed my filthy clothes, and followed the sergeant down the stairs to the bus waiting outside the mission gatehouse.

Ten minutes later I was on the road away from Tung-an and my mission and my Christians.

There were no Christians at the mission gate to see their pastor off. There were no jeering Youth Corps members, nor children to insult me. Two women working in the field on the opposite side of the road did not so much as raise their eyes, so far as I could tell.

Our first stop was the county seat of Ping-lo. A huge crowd gathered around the bus, and followed us, as we walked down the main street toward police headquarters. The soldiers seemed to delight in explaining to the people about my crimes, and what a great spy I had been for the imperialist American government. I was shunted into a cell where a continual line of inquisitive petty officials came to stare at me through the bars of my cage. A large bright light hung in the middle of the cell and remained burning all night. The air outside was filled constantly with propaganda and news broadcasts. Unable to sleep, I tried to reconstruct the horrors of the past two weeks. Compared to those days during Passion Week and Holy Week, the year and a half of previous confinement in my rectory room seemed like a minor illness from which I had long ago recovered.

The judge's words came back to me: "We have obtained all we want from you."

Did he mean that my humiliation before the people and my condemnation by them had achieved the purpose for which the whole drama was staged? If their purpose was to deprive the Christians of Tung-an of their pastor so that the disgraced mission might die, they had, to a certain extent, achieved their evil end. If their purpose was to prove to the people the pernicious designs of the American government against the people of China, they probably had achieved that goal also. America is the dreaded enemy of Communism. And through my ordeal the people were taught that America is such a despicable enemy that it would send a man in the guise of a priest to use religion and medicine as fronts for his vile work of espionage.

I asked myself: "Why will they not understand that the American people and the American government do not in any way wish harm to the people of China?" The answer was long and I was too weary. I knew the answer was not to be found in Tung-an, nor in Peiping. I knew it was to be found in the place from which no truth can be expected to come.

Early the next morning, after a bowl of rice, they marched me back through the mile-long busy street to the bus. The jeers of the students rang in my ears as they shouted: "Down with the American spy!"

It was impossible any longer to carry my blanket and bag.

I dropped them several times, and finally stopped exhausted and sat down. The corporal started to assist me, but the surly sergeant cursed him and said: "That you can't do. He must carry his own things."

I heard the corporal whisper: "If you don't get someone to help him he will never make it."

They ordered a man standing by one of the shops nearby to help me.

Hundreds of "volunteer" soldiers leaving for Korea were milling about the bus terminal. They were naturally curious to see me, and to learn all about my crimes. They were saying: "That's the American devil Chin Peh-teh, whose name has been in the paper so much. Chairman Mao has pardoned him." Pictures of me were constantly being snapped, not only by the short fat man who was still there, making the trip with us, but by every officer who possessed a camera.

The same treatment was given me at Laipo and in Kweilin, the capital and the chief city of our diocese. It was here, fifteen years before, that I had begun my missionary career; and I was saddened to be thus led through the familiar streets as an outcast and criminal. I was weak almost to fainting. I scanned the faces of the mob that lined the main street for someone who would look at and acknowledge me. But all eyes were cast down and no one dared recognize me.

Before I was allowed to use the prison cell assigned to me in Kweilin, I was ordered to sweep it out and clear the hallway leading to it. After that, I was given a bowl of drinking water by the prison guard, but my own guards took it for themselves when they saw it. The sergeant then came into my cell to inform me that in the morning we were to proceed by train from Kweilin north to Henyang and from Henyang out to Canton. Then he warned me: "We are going to trust you now.

Only four guards are assigned to take you to Canton and from there to the border for expulsion." He added again: "Don't at any time open the window of the train. Don't try to jump out of the train at any time." Which seemed to me quite an unnecessary piece of advice since I had no intention *now* of trying to escape, for I had nowhere to escape to but to my death.

During the long, tedious train ride I was forced at each stop to stand on the station platform to be put on exhibition while the guards narrated to the curious mob my crimes and how I was being pardoned by "merciful Mao Tse-tung." In the larger cities loudspeakers screeched out the news of my presence, along with news of the victorious progress of the war in Korea. At each station there was feverish activity. Youth Corps members were there with their banners, as I had seen them so often in Tung-an.

"There's that spy, Chin Peh-teh," was the cry from everyone's lips. I learned, as we went along, that all the newspapers had been printing daily accounts of my spy work with the Legion of Mary.

The city of Henyang was treated to a good look at me as I was dragged along the main street. My weakened condition and my dysentery caused no apparent feeling of sympathy in anyone. As we boarded the train in Henyang, I saw three other foreigners, obviously missionaries who were being expelled as I was. It was the first time in over a year that I had seen someone who would understand my thoughts. If I could only get close enough to talk with them, I thought.

In Canton, swept clean by the political prisoners each day, there were many posters showing Uncle Sam trying to buy Chinese people with American dollars. Billboards urged the people to increase production, and defeat America and aid Korea.

The guards brought me to a hotel room in Canton instead of to the police headquarters. For the first time in almost a month I looked at myself in a mirror, and the shock was terrific. Bearded and gaunt, I looked for some time before I could decide who it was I saw. Fearful that the British authorities might not recognize me, since I was now so different from my passport picture, I asked the guard for some water and some shaving equipment. He refused bluntly and told me to be quiet.

Later three of the guards went out for their evening meal and left me alone with the corporal. I thanked him for his acts of kindness toward me, and he was embarrassed. Then he spoke to me: "Now you are going back to America, and you should work hard for Communism there. Go home and tell the people in America about the glories of Communism. Of course," he added, "you'll have to do it secretly and quietly, as we worked in Southwest China before the Army of Liberation came to our area."

So that was it. I was to join the "peace offensive" in America; I was to study and apply the proper technique for the destruction of my own country.

He continued, "You know the reason merciful Mao has pardoned you is so that you can go on to work for a greater Communist world."

The poor fellow was so dead in earnest. He really felt sorry for me, leaving his "liberated" country for the "chains of capitalism." He actually believed every word he spoke to me and was confident that I was making dutiful mental notes as he described for me the methods he used in his village long before the Party took over. And he cautioned me again on secrecy.

At that moment a noisy torchlight parade went by in front of the hotel. We looked out at the enthusiastic demonstration, and the corporal explained to me that it was a Youth Corps escorting volunteers, as so often happened in Tung-an, who were leaving for the war in Korea to save China from the imperialists.

Next morning two Cantonese police officers and my four guards put me aboard a train for the town of Shum-chun, which is at the boundary line between China and the British leased territory of Kowloon. The guard sitting next to me told the two guards in the seat in back to watch me for a bit. After a moment, a well-dressed young man sat down in the seat made vacant by the guard. He spoke in English: "My name is So-and-So. Are you an American?"

I said, "Yes, an American priest."

Just then the guard in back of me tapped the young man on the shoulder and said: "You are not to talk with this man. He is a prisoner convicted of spying."

The young man smiled back and said, "Don't worry about me. I've had my brain washed, and there is no danger."

He gave me a wink and went on in English: "Look, Father, you are going out now into the freedom of democracy and you are lucky. I must remain here in chains with our fellow countrymen. I have another year of college in Canton and then I must work for the People's Government."

He told me about his admiration for one of our Maryknoll Fathers who had once taught him in a university in Canton, and he asked me sadly to remember him to this priest. When the guard returned, the young man left me. Later he returned with a cup of tea for me, and I thanked him in spite of the growls of the guard.

At the border all the passengers were lined up for inspection. I went to fall in line, but was rudely pushed off to one side and told to wait. I waited for at least two hours after the last passenger had gone through the small opening in the barbed-wire fence. I began to think that this was another part of the endless ordeal, to let me look across into the free air of the British possession and see the British soldiers there, and then to return me for execution. Several times I approached the officials but they impatiently waved me back. Just when it seemed that I could stand it no longer, one of the guards gave me the signal to move toward the barbed wire.

I staggered through the opening and once on the other side I began wandering around in circles. One of the British soldiers came up to me and took me by the shoulders, and for the first time in a year and a half I heard a voice full of sympathy and kindness: "It's okay, Father. Everything will be all right now. Come with us, you're free now," he said. And I wept as he held me in his strong arms.

It is difficult to put in words one's feelings on being released. To be so near to death and escape, to have an end come at last to a long torturing nightmare . . . it is no exaggeration to say that the very air seemed different where I was now standing—even though it was but fifty feet away from the "Bamboo Curtain." My mind seemed to be clearing up, and some strength was returning to my limbs.

My emotions were a jumble—thanksgiving to Our Lady for seeing me through the ordeal; disbelief that it could be true; joy at being free; sorrow at knowing that my helpless Christians and the Sisters were still there still among those fiendish zealots, going about seeking whom they might devour; and sorrow, too, that the desecration of the Church was not local to Tung-an, but universal throughout the whole of China. I felt sorrow for and pride in the heroic Chinese priests, so many already martyred, so many rotting in prison. They will be beacons encouraging the faithful to ride out this mighty storm.

This much I know—many of those mountain people of mine around Tung-an are waiting for me to return. They are saying their rosaries still though they may have no beads on which to count the Aves. If, through the aid of Our Lady of China, we are able to return any time within the next ten or twenty years, Christians will greet us on their knees with tears of joy. If we have to wait longer than twenty years, we may have to start near the beginning again, this time not to make some Chinese Christians, but to make all China Christian!

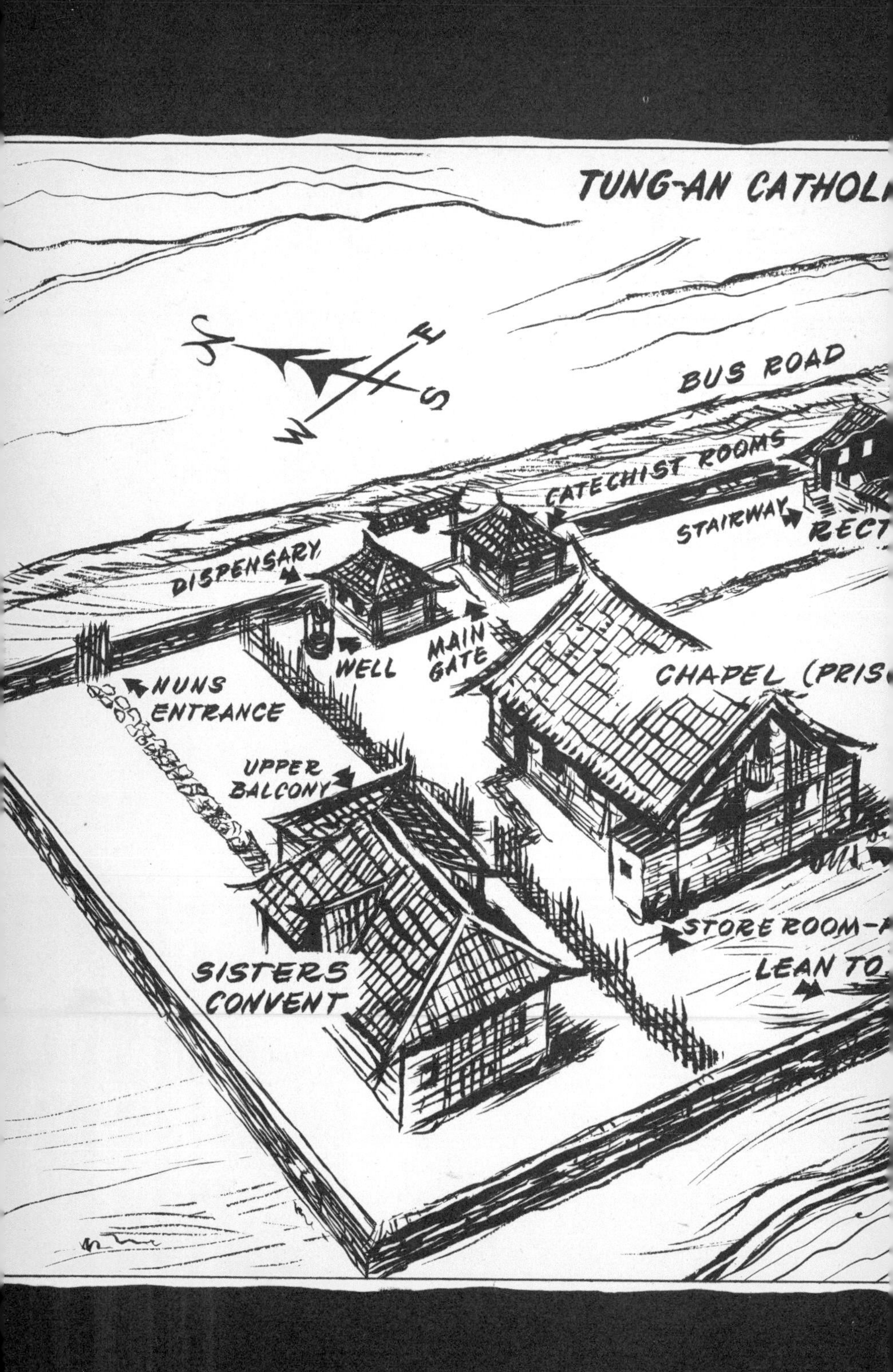
TUNG-AN CATHOL
BUS ROAD
CATECHIST ROOMS
STAIRWAY
RECT
DISPENSARY
MAIN GATE
WELL
NUNS ENTRANCE
CHAPEL (PRIS
UPPER BALCONY
STORE ROOM-
LEAN TO
SISTERS CONVENT